RESPONSE TO THE RELUCTANT SHAMAN

Reading this book brought the same flood of insight I experienced as Bernard Morin's student nearly two decades ago. The energy from his extraordinary personal stories literally leaps off every page. Once again, he has inspired me to explore the unseen forces operating in my life — forces that continue to bring me deep personal awareness, learning, and hope. I am reminded that far from being something to be feared, shamanic experiences are gifts that can not only heal us, but also call us to become healers ourselves. This book is for anyone who has felt the pull to nurture their own innate powers of intuition. It opens a door to those seeking greater meaning, wholeness, connection to nature, and spiritual discovery.

— MICHAEL CHAVEZ, CO-AUTHOR OF *REHUMANIZING LEADERSHIP: PUTTING PURPOSE BACK INTO BUSINESS*

Bernard's a gifted teacher, healer, person who exemplifies honesty, love, and compassion in all he does. Upset by not having even one out of fifteen shamanic journeys in his class, he comforted me by saying, "Don't worry, it's right there." And, it did happen, later. That's how he approaches everyone he meets … with love and compassion … and it just oozes from these book pages.

— TAMARA MICHAEL, WORLD TRAVELLER, AUTHOR, *THE SUITCASE WIFE*

Simply put, Bernard Morin's work is transformative. In this long-awaited collection of personal stories, *The Reluctant Shaman* invites the reader to accompany him on his journey of extraordinary connections with the seen and the unseen. It is a must-read that encourages us to face our biggest fears and step into our most authentic selves.

— ELSPETH JONES, ARTIST, BUSINESS CONSULTANT, HEALER, MYSTIC

THE RELUCTANT SHAMAN

An Urban Mystic's Journey

BERNARD MORIN

LIBRARY AND ARCHIVES CANADA CATALOGUING IN PUBLICATION

Title: The reluctant shaman: An urban mystic's journey / by Bernard Morin.
Names: Morin, Bernard, author.
ISBN 978-1-7390-771-0-5 (SOFTCOVER) | ISBN 978-1-7390-771-1-2 (HTML)

PERMISSIONS

Permissions have been obtained from the Buckminster Fuller estate for the quotes within this book. The first quote in the opening pages by R. Buckminster Fuller from *I Seem to Be a Verb*, (1970). The quote by R. Buckminster Fuller in the chapter called "Responsibility" is attributed but unverifiable at the time of publication.

Logo design and illustrations: Greg Curtis
Cover image/design & Interior text design: Tannice Goddard, tannicegdesigns.ca

Contact: Bernard Morin
www.inthenameofhealing.ca

I live on Earth at present, and I don't know what I am. I know that I am not a category. I am not a thing — a noun. I seem to be a verb, an evolutionary process — an integral function of the universe.

— R. BUCKMINSTER FULLER, *I SEEM TO BE A VERB*, (1970)

CONTENTS

PREFACE

EVERYTHING STATED HERE, WITH a few acknowledged exceptions, comes directly from my own life. As I move into advanced age, I have felt an increased responsibility to pass along my accumulated knowledge. It ultimately becomes a matter of responsibility to the greater good. What I have grown to appreciate as I write, are the reminders of the wisdom of my suppressed authentic self. That alone has been worth the effort.

I AM A FASCINATED OBSERVER of life though I am not an exceptionally intelligent person nor scholarly in my pursuit of knowledge … quite the opposite in fact. I am naïve, overly trusting, often openly emotional until recent years and of average mental and intellectual ability. My compensating abilities are a highly developed intuitive sense coupled with emotional intelligence and a lack of cynical pre-judgment. I believe that almost anything is possible if it is for our highest good or for the people we serve.

What I have observed with the work I do is rapid, emotional healing that can lead to spiritual growth. Trauma that traditionally would take a lengthy time to work through can be moved out of the body's memory very quickly. I don't make this claim lightly. It works. I know of very few people for whom it was not successful.

Buried trauma can be brought into consciousness where it can then be released with relative ease.

It has been a privilege both to witness and to assist this in others. It does not work for everything though. Seizures, and other neurological disorders, advanced tumours or joint deterioration, birth defects and advanced disease forms are all beyond reach in my experience. What I can offer in these situations is calm, and in many cases … acceptance.

What follows are a series of stories that describe how my learning came to me as each awareness unfolded. They aren't chronologically organized but are grouped together to illuminate the teachings I experienced and the sense of spirituality that resulted. I have not spent time investigating alternative religions or spirituality nor do I follow any formal mode of religiosity. I am adamant about not polluting my own truth with the experience and beliefs of others.

My hope is that these stories, when read … slowly … and deliberately … will bathe you in the permission you seek to lead the life you are intended to follow. Take all the time you need. Everything that follows here is a true account of my life's events.

Shaman and healer are not words I am comfortable using to describe myself, though they are partial descriptors. A Shaman is most broadly used as an indigenous identifier. The term 'healer' might infer that the healer is the source agent of the healing. From my experience, the energy that is vital to assisting the body to rectify itself, is simply channeled through the healer directly to the client. A 'catalyst' for healing is yet another possibility.

I believe that your community acknowledges whatever terms suit you. Nonetheless, it's a high honour and comes with an even higher sense of responsibility. The term I would choose for myself is 'mystic', yet even that is not a well-understood term and doesn't fully cover who I am. I am absorbed with experiencing the inexplicable, the misunderstood, the mysteries that surround us. A mystic cheerleader would seem more apt yet that conjures up images of pom poms and football games in Mystic River, Massachusetts. You see the difficulty.

As you may then assume, answering the often-posed question of what I do for a living is therefore very complicated for me. I usually say simply that I am retired, 'at liberty' if you will. People only find out about my work through word-of-mouth. Otherwise, I am happy existing under the radar.

IN THE WISDOM OF hindsight, my life has been an enormous gift.

PARIS, FRANCE

MY FIRST OFFICIAL EMPLOYMENT AT Expo '67 had just come to an end and at twenty-two, I was ripe for an adventure. On a cheap one-way flight to Paris in November, I set out my intention for the trip. I have English and French heritage, so I was intrigued to explore both sides of my cultural background. From the age of seventeen I was drawn to the worlds of art and theatre, so I was determined to seek that out as well. I wanted to know about a life of riches and excess but also, in contrast, a simple and hard-scrabble existence.

Less than two weeks later, I landed inside a French novel.

IT WAS WINTER IN PARIS, though not as extreme as I was used to. I watched as a light snow paralyzed traffic. When a light turned green, five cars would spin their wheels in unison, barely moving. When the light turned red, the same five cars would slowly drift across the intersection. People were afraid to walk anywhere. A particular quietude descended across the city.

Paris was both an assault on the senses and a gift. I was at first swept away by the mélange of scents. Diesel exhaust coupled with an almost acrid tinge of what must have been brake dust, but I swear I could detect the scent of gunpowder. The wafting humid aura surrounding the Seine was laced with traces of French perfume, espresso, sewage and unexpectedly … flowers.

I was swept away by the attention to design in every architectural detail I saw. Every bridge, railing, doorway, Metro entrance, grill and pedestal exuded attention of the utmost consciousness. The presence of a protected and revered culture was everywhere. I saw it in the streetsweepers with their twig brooms every morning, bundles of baguettes standing in doorways of shops that were not yet open for the day. Oceans of flowers I had never seen before were exhibited near Metro entrances. Foodstuffs and bon bons, exquisitely displayed, were completely foreign to my experience and entranced me particularly in the windows of Fauchon. I would stare at them wondering if I would ever be able to afford such delicate pieces of culinary art.

I was in an architectural and historical fairyland. I would walk through the side streets of the West Bank and look up at the pock-marked walls that bore witness to a Resistance Movement in the last great War. Layers of history were alive and present if I took the time to sense and to feel them.

I shared a hotel room in the West Bank with four friends who all worked at Expo '67, though that was all we had in common. Their idea of a good time was to buy a cheap bottle of table wine, a baguette, some cheese and get drunk in the hotel room. I would leave them and wander along Boulevard Saint-Germain to Café Flore or Deux Magots just to watch the people and to listen to them speaking. How did they dress? How did they conduct themselves in public that differed from my upbringing? I bought a trench coat, dress pants and shoes so that I would be less visible as a foreigner in that cosmopolitan universe. I toured Les Halles at four in the morning to watch the trucks roll in with their produce and animal carcasses, a working girl in every doorway smoking a cigarette, their smoke blended with cheap perfume and a hint of urine from the pissoirs. At night I would walk through backstreets and then stop to watch the rats that would emerge from the decorative grillwork that annotated the base of every tree. A subtle noise or a motor scooter would cause them the disappear in mere seconds. They were the invisible stagehands behind the curtain that was the splendor of Paris.

It was intoxicating. I was in a novel by Rimbaud or Flaubert. Who needed wine?

Through a friend I 'happened' to run into there, I was introduced to a sculptor whose work captivated me. I voiced my appreciation. He appeared to be impressed that a "Canadian" could understand his work. Why exactly, I didn't ask, sensing it would be a social smear on my citizenship. But as it turned out, he was looking for an assistant, albeit unpaid … but room and board were included.

I appeared to fit the bill. I moved into his small, fourth floor, Napoleonic-era flat which doubled as his studio.

The main window had four glass panes of which two were broken. The only source of heat was a barely functioning electric coil heater. I managed the cold by wearing my bathing suit and a light sweater in the morning then as the day progressed, adding pants, heavy socks, a t-shirt and then a long-sleeved shirt under the sweater. By bedtime I would finally be warm enough to fall asleep in my sleeping bag on the clay tile floor.

There was no sink (kitchen or otherwise), but surprisingly there was a square bathtub. The communal toilet was built into a corner of the building's stairwell over a hole in the floor with no light and no means of locking the flimsy greenboard door … a remnant of the sanitation improvements from the Napoleonic Era.

The 'cookstove' was a metal grill fixed over a propane tank, not uncommon in France. There was no refrigerator nor cupboards.

Food was never plentiful, but the sculptor had a plan. He had affairs with very wealthy women who put him through art school and would bring food when they 'visited'. I would then go for long walks. When I returned there would be baguette, cheeses, fine chocolate, pastries and wine which were quickly wrapped up for another day. Food kept for three or four days especially if we put it outside onto the roof of the adjoining building in the cool winter air.

On one occasion, I accompanied the sculptor on an afternoon visit to the home of one of his 'special' women.

We were served champagne and caviar in the salon.

I was agog at the ostentatious wealth. Velvet-covered walls with Louis XVI gold sconces, five enormous floral arrangements in the 'salon' alone, Chinese antique carpets on top of broadloom, a gold, nautilus shell-shaped tub in the bathroom. It was opulence beyond my imaginings. The contradiction in economic status was not lost on me.

WORKING ALONGSIDE THE SCULPTOR, WHOSE name I have decided to protect given the nature of what I am about to divulge, I had the opportunity to assist in the installation of the first kinetic flower displays for the spring collection at an haute couture house on Avenue Matignon. We worked in the middle of the night in great secrecy. One night, I was crouched in the window at about 3 am working on the installation when a knock broke through the night silence behind me. I turned my head to take in a vision of a clown in full costume and make-up wiggling his fingers at me and smiling. It felt like a dream. I recognized that what I was now doing had nothing in common with my formal education, with the exception of my modest ability to get by in French.

THE SPRING WINDOW INSTALLATION WAS an enormous success. Within two weeks almost every fashion house in Paris had installed kinetic flowers in their Spring windows, thus the need for secrecy.

So much for Parisian originality.

THE SCULPTOR HAD ARRANGED TO have me photographed on the Champs Elysée with an eye to getting me work as a model. I was also introduced to a woman with whom I might have an affair. She would pay for my keep and any courses I chose to pursue.

A noose of expectation was tightening around my neck.

MY FORAY INTO PARIS ALL came to an end after one awkward evening of drinks at the George V. I was there as the assistant to the sculptor along with two powerful women, one of whom was a fashion house executive, the other the wife of a prominent politician. Their secretaries acted as silent witnesses.

The sculptor was being set up with the politician's wife who could then get him commissions to do monuments. She was also a known nymphomaniac, so flirting was in order, but no sex … or it was over.

Meanwhile, I was being heavily flirted with because, get this, Canadian boys were rumoured to be virgins longer than most.

There followed much pinching of bums.

I WAS GROWING MORE UNCOMFORTABLE by the minute. Contraceptives were illegal in France at the time though you wouldn't know it by peering into the waters of the Seine each morning. But these same privileged women would check themselves into hospitals for abortions whenever their husbands were out-of-town. It was a way of life in France.

Finally, after a few hours, I had witnessed enough. I bolted, quietly excusing myself, and returned to the studio apartment. I packed up my meagre belongings and left for London in the middle of the night.

I am not proud of the way I exited but I knew my work for the sculptor was finished and the social scene was overwhelming.

AS I SAT ON THE overnight train to the Channel ferry, I mused about the outcome of my intentions. I experienced everything I set out to experience save one, the theatre. Was that all strictly coincidence? Did I make that happen? Does this happen to other people?

London, as it turned out, held even more answers for me.

NOTTING HILL GATE, LONDON, 1968

LONDON, ANOTHER CULTURAL BRUSH WITH fate. Within two weeks of arriving, I managed to once more land an unpaid job, this time at an avant-garde theatre in Notting Hill Gate, a rehearsal space for the Ballet Rambert. My remaining intention had now been realized.

The theatre brought in small international touring stage productions such as you might see off-off-Broadway. Eventually, I was 'offered' the position of stage-manager for which I was grossly under-qualified but at a salary of 2 pounds, 10 shillings a week. I am not sure there was a line-up for the position.

There I was, scaling rickety ladders to the full height of a very high ceiling while carrying a large theatre light crooked under one arm. The building was cold, dirty and had minimal facilities … but I loved every bizarre minute of it.

The incoming theatre productions were ground-breaking for the times. Live chickens and goats on stage; a woman dressed in strips of transparent shower curtains and nothing else; a nude woman whom I had to catch in a theatre curtain as she exited off stage through a fire door directly onto the street. Two of the plays were by Lanford Wilson, staged by the American Theatre Project.

One play, "The Madness Of Lady Bright," was about an aging, demented drag queen who kept count of his/her tricks by having them sign the bedroom wall. While the other play, "Home Free," was about a brother who had agoraphobia and a rampant imagination but was completely dependent upon his sister for his existence. I recalled reading a review of "Home Free" in Time magazine when I was in University. It featured a picture of Michael Warren Powell, one of the two leads with a very positive prediction for his future, I remember wondering at the time if I would ever meet him. Here he was on our stage in London while I was stage manager. What manner of coincidence is that?

IT WAS THE LATE 1960's. London was bustling with Carnaby Street, Mary Quant, Portobello Market and Biba's all to the soundtrack of the Beatles' "Lucy In The Sky With Diamonds". Biba's appeared to be the future of department store retail.

Everywhere I looked there was another new experience.

Priceless antique cars, the likes of which I had never seen, were parked innocuously in driveways. Small yet perfect homes were built into Mews which had formerly been stables and back lanes. Thresholds and windowsills were made of stone not wood. Older residences were well-preserved and occupied. They weren't demolished and replaced with ranch bungalows nor were they renovated with picture windows.

I came across a pet cemetery in a park nearby with small headstones inscribed with names such as Nigel, Angel, Millicent and Bruiser. People often walked or took the Tube or the double-decker buses. The automobile was considered a bit of a luxury and were often parked bumper-to-bumper on the street for days on end. Our suburbs were deserts by comparison. Paris seemed more fluid and artful next to London. There seemed to be an inherent yet invisible starchiness in the way life proceeded in London unless you were in the theatre, music or fashion, those bulkheads of radicalized behaviour and appearance.

The fashion of the day was trending there like wildfire. Rock stars drove Rolls-Royces and wore big floppy velvet hats. The images of Twiggy and Jean Shrimpton in mini skirts and white vinyl boots dominated the media. Peter Max was the God of image artwork. And, everywhere I looked, hormones were flashing like lightening.

Canada was a rapidly fading memory in black and white.

I HAD RENTED A BED-SITTER near the theatre for exactly 2 pounds, 10 shillings a week which was my entire salary. I had a sink, hot water, a two-burner hotplate and a single bed. The outside windowsill doubled as my cooler. The bathroom was in the hallway with a toilet and bathtub shared with three other tenants.

It was all I needed. The residence was located near an intersection where two busy streets converged. In order to buy food, I took a job making beds and cleaning a student hostel in Holland Park. I was able to buy a piece of chicken once a week and vegetables when they were on sale at Jimmy Paces' across the street. I saved the bones for making soup. I learned to love Brussel sprouts and parsnips which were always a bargain. It was hand-to-mouth living which, as I recalled, I had also asked to experience. Coming from a family home where there was always food for three growing boys, it was therefore my challenge to figure out how to exist on minimal sustenance.

ONE MORNING AS I WAS waiting to catch a bus across the street, I noticed an elderly lady, shoulders hunched, clutching a shopping bag with obvious determination. I had seen her there a few times.

She stood well out into the thoroughfare on the raised curb that separated the lanes of traffic. There she was angrily shaking her finger at the traffic as it moved quickly and insensitively past her, though occasionally, an obliging motorist would honk his horn to further agitate her.

She fascinated me. I couldn't imagine what it must be like to be her, to be in her body with the courage to stand there day after day publicly displaying her anger without any hint of embarrassment. In an attempt to access a more compassionate understanding, I decided to mimic her but from a discrete distance obscured by a light standard.

When I felt I had her stance down, I waited until I returned home later in the day, then I assumed her demeanor. I paced around my room wagging my finger as she did. Within several minutes, it came to me. I knew what she was about.

She had been raised in a family where children were to be seen but not heard. She had an abusive father who ruled the house with an iron fist. Consequently, there she was out on Chepstow Place at Westbourne Grove every day shaking her fist at him.

I was shocked that I knew so much by simply taking on her posture but I was now more curious than ever.

I discovered later that her name was Mary and local residents would slip a ten shilling note into her bag when they encountered her. I loved that about London. People still cared for each other.

WALKING AROUND THE CITY, I would follow people who had an unusual gait until I could replicate it. Again, back in my room the emotional references for their gait came to me in just a few minutes. I then experimented with intuiting the interesting faces of people from across the street. To my complete amazement I was able to tune in to their emotional histories even at a considerable distance. All I needed to do was to express the intention. But ... what did that mean? Was it a universal observation or some fluke I had stumbled upon? Was I invading their private worlds? Had I crossed some invisible line?

I started meeting up with a friend, an aspiring actress named Diana Chappell, who shared the same fascination. She had been working as a nurse's aide and had started to notice that patients who had similar physical issues had almost identical emotional issues or circumstances. Diana and I met every two weeks to compare our observations.

On one notable occasion, Diana burst into my room and said:

"I have it. The legs are about career."

I agreed but I felt strongly that the left leg was about the career environment or upbringing and the right leg was about career and will. Yet how I knew, I couldn't say.

We agreed to keep our eyes open for confirmation over the following two weeks. But the very next day, when I opened the newspaper, there it was.

Both Richard Nixon and General Franco of Spain had medical issues with their left legs. Both were in political turmoil.

Can it be that simple, I wondered?

More importantly, my passion had now been fully launched.

I HAVE SINCE BECOME AWARE that this technique of mimicry is employed by both actors and dancers. It enables them to connect more deeply with characters they portray. It is an extraordinary tool and is one I feel blessed to have simply fallen into.

AROUND 1972, BACK IN CANADA and on my way to work in advertising each morning, I would walk to the streetcar stop and always seemed to have pain develop in my right knee as I reached one specific corner. I assumed I had a physical knee issue that was causing pain after an amount of effort.

One day on the way to work but completely lost in thought, I noticed I was well past that corner and yet had no knee pain. Immediately, the pain in my knee returned. Damn, it was all in my head…or was it? But…why was it happening?

In truth, I wasn't busy enough at the agency where I worked. We had engaged in no new business pitches which always involved me. I was considering leaving but was conflicted around the issues of employer loyalty and career advancement. Consequently, I twiddled my thumbs at my desk most days and was quite bored. But as soon as I decided that I had to leave, the knee pain left me entirely. I had received and fully embraced the message. Knee problems seem to be exacerbated by indecision.

However, that first position in advertising taught me how to communicate. In hindsight it became crucial to my sense of self. I had no trouble envisioning but words and the expression of rational thought did not come easily. I had to put real effort into finding the words to express myself clearly.

ADVERTISING ALSO TAUGHT ME WHO I wasn't.

AT ABOUT THE SAME TIME, I noticed that my hands seemed to possess a knowledge of their own. If someone had a sore shoulder, I instinctively knew where to place a finger to relax the specific muscle. Initially, I figured this was simply my party trick, but I underestimated it. An ability was now surfacing (or was it re-surfacing) within me and was about to be brought out in full force.

My eyes always tell me where my attention needs to be placed. I will catch myself staring at someone, then my consciousness will slowly realize that I was being shown something or someone in need of healing or perhaps there was something I needed to learn there. I admit it got me into some embarrassing situations and made others quite uncomfortable, but it begs the question of where my consciousness was when my eyes were so fixed. Nonetheless, I had to teach myself to be more discreet about it.

I had to learn to control the autonomy to which my eyes were connected … in other words, I had to suppress my instinct.

REGRETFULLY, I LOST TOUCH WITH Diana after I returned to Canada, yet our initial observations would be confirmed almost word-for-word 20 years later when I was introduced to Louise Hay's work. The diagrams that follow on the next 3 pages, detail how I learned to interpret problems in the body. It is still relevant today.

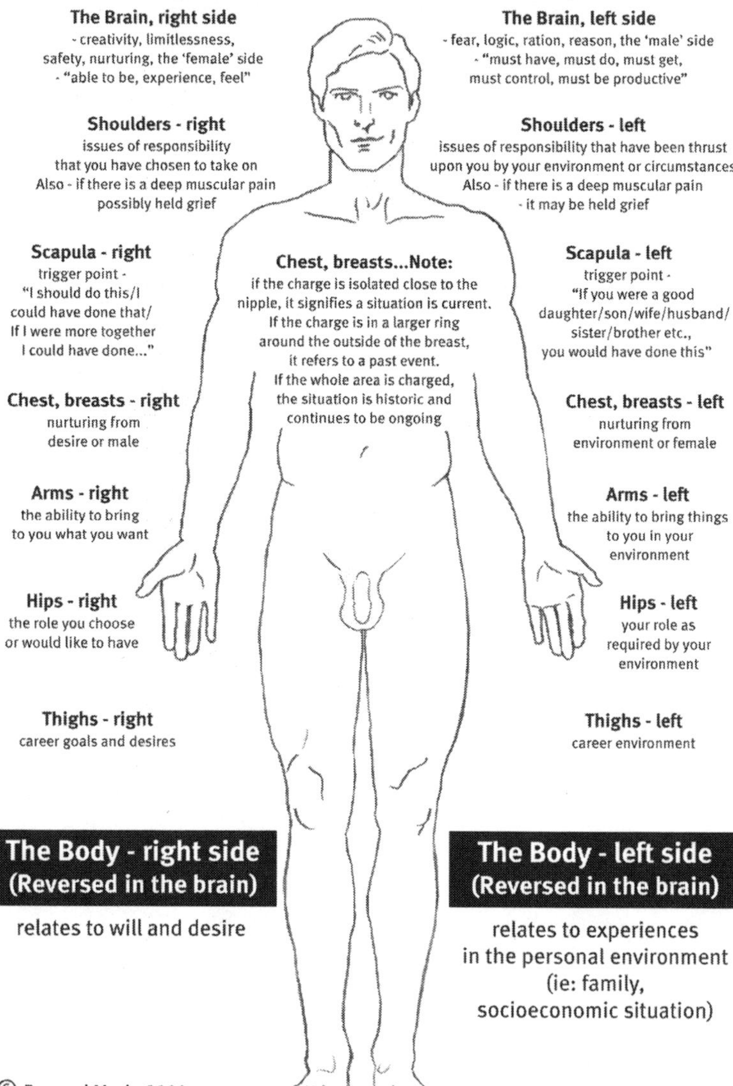
How to Read Parts of the Body
The Brain, right side
- creativity, limitlessness, safety, nurturing, the 'female' side - "able to be, experience, feel"
The Brain, left side
- fear, logic, ration, reason, the 'male' side - "must have, must do, must get, must control, must be productive"
Shoulders - right
issues of responsibility that you have chosen to take on Also - if there is a deep muscular pain possibly held grief
Shoulders - left
issues of responsibility that have been thrust upon you by your environment or circumstances Also - if there is a deep muscular pain - it may be held grief
Scapula - right
trigger point - "I should do this/I could have done that/ If I were more together I could have done..."
Chest, breasts...Note:
if the charge is isolated close to the nipple, it signifies a situation is current. If the charge is in a larger ring around the outside of the breast, it refers to a past event. If the whole area is charged, the situation is historic and continues to be ongoing
Scapula - left
trigger point - "If you were a good daughter/son/wife/husband/ sister/brother etc., you would have done this"
Chest, breasts - right
nurturing from desire or male
Chest, breasts - left
nurturing from environment or female
Arms - right
the ability to bring to you what you want
Arms - left
the ability to bring things to you in your environment
Hips - right
the role you choose or would like to have
Hips - left
your role as required by your environment
Thighs - right
career goals and desires
Thighs - left
career environment
The Body - right side (Reversed in the brain)
relates to will and desire
The Body - left side (Reversed in the brain)
relates to experiences in the personal environment (ie: family, socioeconomic situation)
© Bernard Morin 2022

How to Read Parts of the Body (Con't)

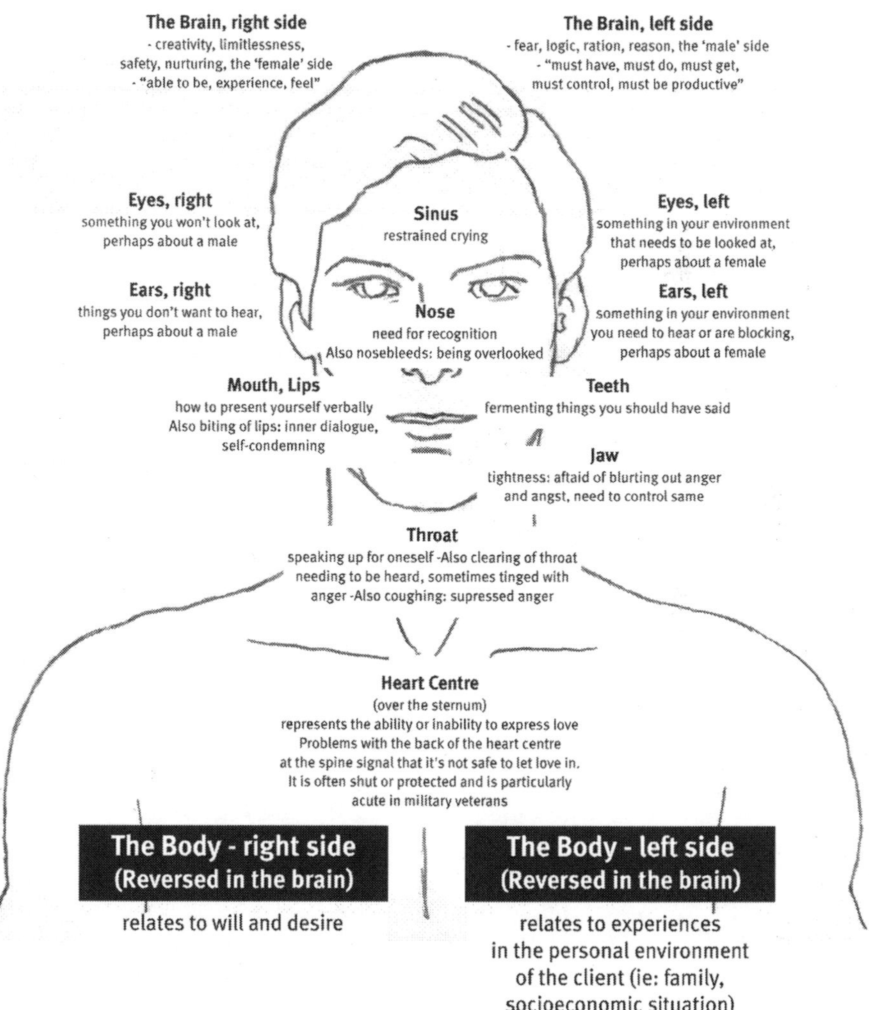

How to Read Parts of the Body (Con't)

The Body, right side
relates to will and desire (reversed in the brain)

The Body, left side
relates to experiences in the personal environment of the client (ie: family, socioeconomic situation)

Neck
the battleground between the head and the body, or between the conscious and the unconscious, thus headaches

Upper Back
Who's on your back?

Lungs
represent the freedom to experience life. The lower lung signals fear and thus causes shallow breathing. Large chest cavities can also signal a need to be brave and put on a strong front

Joints, Elbows
the ease with which you feel you can bring things to you - also pain, anxiety about your ability to bring things

Stomach
anger you've swallowed and not expressed. Centre of self-esteem

Arms - left
the ability to bring things to you in your environment

Arms - right
the ability to bring to you what you want

Liver
a place of old stored anger and despair

Pancreas
bitterness, no sweetness left, controlled anger with self, often coupled with a denied need to control others.

Kidneys
represent the ability to filter out negativity in what you think (right side) or in what you perceive in your environment

Intestines
represent your ability to assimilate whatever life brings you, what to discard and to trust in the flow of life

Sexual Area
Centre of personal power or powerlessness

Hands/Fingers
effectiveness or the perceived inability to be effective - conflict between your perceived responsibility and your...

Bladder
Irritability, a belief that things won't work out for the best

Legs
represent the ease of movement through life

Knees
represent flexibility

Calves
represent the power you put into decisions about movement forward or career mobility

Skin
how you present yourself, the ego (cross reference with the area of the body in which difficulties arise)

Feet
the ability to articulate your decision and movement

A FATALITY OF SECRETS

FROM THE VANTAGE POINT OF hindsight, being born into fear has been a certain blessing. I can never remember a period in my young life when I wasn't fearful. When I look at photos of me at age two, the fear is already there. I knew I was different and yet somehow, I was acutely aware that it wasn't safe to talk about it.

I felt like a foreigner. I also had a strong sense of impending danger.

I had been stitched into a body that was too tight for me and wouldn't respond with the ease of coordination I witnessed in my peers. I also experienced a "white noise" in my head that sounded like a short-wave radio between stations. It was constant and disruptive. I had to learn to shut it down or at least distract myself from it.

Additionally, "things" were happening that I had no control over. From about the age of three, I was having alien abduction experiences at night when I went to bed. Perhaps this was the source of my dread and terror. These incidents re-occurred throughout my childhood, into my teens then stopped until one re-occurrence when I was fifty-one. The late Dolores Cannon's book "The Custodians" details identical experiences in her clients, but more on this a bit later.

THE COST

MY MOTHER CAME DOWN WITH polio when I was seven. This was 1952. She had three young children, I was the oldest. My youngest brother was only eighteen months. Mum's condition did not require an iron lung but she lost full co-ordination in one leg, her lower back and one wrist. To her credit, she was a fighter and my Father was a prince of a man who rose to the challenge. This was before Medicare was instituted in Canada, so my parents were left with enormous hospital bills for the times.

We (the children) were taken into my Father's siblings homes in Ottawa, a considerable drive away and in retrospect, at great risk to their own children. My Mother recovered enough to be out of hospital after five months. My Father drove her to Ottawa to reunite with us … but regrettably, I didn't recognize the woman on crutches who got out of the car. She was a stranger, she had changed so much physically. The fact that she was with my Father just added to my confusion. I can't imagine how devastated she felt.

I still feel her sadness.

I ARRIVED HOME ALONG WITH my younger brother a few weeks later. The very next morning, he was hospitalized with viral pneumonia.

My youngest brother came home a few days afterward. My Father had to take a job on the road to make sufficient money to cover all the medical bills. We had also changed houses and therefore neighbourhoods. Everything had changed.

Chaos was now the theme in our young world.

My mother's bed was fitted with pulleys that allowed her to sit up. At times she was placed on the couch where she stayed for hours until an adult could check on her.

We went to school as usual, but the neighbourhood children weren't allowed to play with us for fear they would catch Polio, then known as Infantile Paralysis. Friends of my parents would no longer visit or even call us. Family was our only social lifeline.

Additionally, an anonymous man would call our phone and stay silent for several minutes a few times a day. I was beginning to feel paranoid. Was he watching us? Did he know us?

With my Father away from Monday to Friday, one of my aunts said to me "You're the man of the house now."

What did that mean? I was seven … and very confused.

I started by making breakfast for my brothers and my Mother. I was her hands and support during the week but on weekends when my Father came home, I was jobless.

I wasn't a kid and I clearly wasn't yet an adult. As a seven-year-old … my sense of self was already compromised.

Playing seemed frivolous and was at odds with what appeared to be expected of me. Life was suddenly very serious.

AS A RESULT OF THAT experience, I now realize, I lost any sense of confidence and most importantly of playfulness.

My childhood had become collateral damage.

The ultimate loss has been that I couldn't relate to children. In fact, they terrified me. I couldn't be playful nor encourage carefree lives. It somehow felt dangerous and irresponsible. I lost an ability to connect to and to play with nephews and nieces when they came along, any children in fact until they reached adulthood. This has been devastating for me and most importantly, for them. I mourn the lost opportunity to build a sense of being loved and to encourage them to be spontaneously the young people they truly could be. In that respect, I feel I have failed as an adult.

THE ALIENS

AS A VERY YOUNG CHILD, ages 3 to 7, I would at times be awakened from sleep by a very bright light shining in through the venetian blinds of my window. My most vivid memory is from around the age of five. My body was paralyzed. The only parts of me I could move were my eyes. I had no voice. I already knew what was about to happen and I was terrified.

THE LIGHT FROM THE WINDOW silhouetted an androgenous figure positioned at the end of my bed. A nuclear alarm called Terror was now raging though my body.

My next recollection was standing on a narrow, raised stage in a large, darkened space with a curved ceiling, lined up with several other people who were similarly paralyzed. Backlit and moving about below the stage were short, odd-looking beings. They match drawings I have seen of 'Greys' though their faces weren't visible to me. I have no recollection of sound. They were inserting a long needle-like instrument into our groins and genitals. Yet, there was no pain, just the horror of their actions. This, as I realized much later in my life, was likely the source of my vasovagal response, a fear of needles and IV ports, which seems to be common among abductees.

MY NEXT RECOLLECTION WAS BACK in my bed. I had absolutely no sensation of the length of time I was 'out', but the bright light was now gone. My body felt as if a foaming drain-cleaner was running though my veins. I feared that I might explode. Not wanting to create a mess for my parents to clean up, I would gather my blankets, wrap myself up in them and hide in the bottom of my closet.

In the morning, I remember once telling my Mother about the visitation and the look on her face said everything. Don't talk about it. It also created hypervigilance and an almost hysterical undertone in my psyche.

I MUST BE CRAZY

ABOUT THIS TIME, I DISCOVERED that I could cause a wall to respond as if it were a liquid, with ripples running across it. I could also see energy, much like smoke, rising from fresh fruit and flowers. All the objects and features in a room were defined by a bluish, blurry edge that extended outward about two inches. Yet, no-one else I mentioned it to seemed to notice. I assumed it was poor vision on my part. I also knew I was attracted to boys and not to girls.

And … I knew for sure that I could fly.

THE AWARENESS I GAINED FROM those experiences was that the life we are told about isn't all there is. It's far more extensive and brimming with mystery … and fear. Given what I was dealing with, I just assumed that I must be completely crazy. Investigating the abduction experience triggers enormous trauma for some abductees. There still exists a black 'block' or wall that prevents me from accessing the full truth and detail of that experience.

I would comfort myself with the belief that I must be "Other," so that I couldn't expect there to be anyone else like me. It made relating to others almost impossible, an issue that is common in alien abductees who often become societal hermits and loners.

IN ORDER TO SURVIVE AND to avoid being put into a mental institution, my sole focus became to masquerade as a normal person. I had to watch what I said, how I said it, and how I handled myself physically. Every part of my life was now under scrutiny.

I look back on my childhood and see the strength and the courage I must have had to be able to survive everything that was happening to me. In retrospect, I lost myself to the hiding.

As a very fearful, gay man I had a lot at stake in attempting to remain as normal in demeanor as possible. The recommended therapy for my 'disorder' in my teen years was electric shock treatment and an early form of conversion therapy sanctioned by the psychiatric community. It has only been since 1969 in Canada that I am no longer considered a criminal. Yet, a lot of prejudice still existed, notably in the advertising and the film businesses in which I found myself. Plus, I had never been a bright student academically nor was I streetwise, but I did manage to squeak through university.

I experienced great difficulty studying from books. I could read for twenty minutes at most before the lines started to run together at angles. My attention would begin to wander into space. I would catch myself after several minutes and would return to reading … but my attention would skip out at exactly the same place each time. I was so frustrated by the process that I would slam the book against my forehead to wake up my brains, but, of course, it never worked.

I then decided to study in twenty-minute segments with a break in between. But nothing I read seemed to be connecting directly to my memory. History, especially, was anathema to me. It wasn't until years later that I would discover that history was relevant when seen through the eyes of the people who lived it. I could then sense their whole experience and not just a sequence of meaningless dates, articles of governance, decrees, religious dogma and war.

All I really acquired at university was the awareness that I was capable of learning to an officially acknowledged level. However, I felt more at home immersing myself in the abstract paintings of Claude Breeze at the University's McIntosh Gallery.

THE EDUCATION SYSTEM WASN'T AND still isn't geared to support people like me. Given the times we live in, it isn't surprising. I'm not sure how we could assist young people having similar experiences within the current education system though an answer may be found in our First Nations. Their communities are more sensitive to this awareness than is mainstream non-native society.

My parents had a dream for me that included University and a steady job with a detergent manufacturer or perhaps in insurance. Highest on their list of desirable careers was a solid job with a guaranteed pension. Given my own parents' limited education and employment, it wasn't surprising. They had no experience in dealing with my issues and situation.

However, my own unique life wasn't written in the books I was required to study nor was it represented in those kinds of employment. I couldn't tell that to my parents. They had invested heavily both financially and emotionally in my education at a time when money wasn't that plentiful for them. They were doing what they felt was right for me and were offering me an opportunity they didn't have growing up. I couldn't disappoint them.

However, I sensed, correctly, that my life skills would await me elsewhere. Where exactly and what they were, I had no idea.

A VISION AND A DIRECTION

BY THE LATE 1980'S, AND in advertising for over 15 years, I was seeing Ruth, a therapist who was very spiritually aware. My 'cover' was starting to tear at the seams especially in the glare of the spotlight on AIDS. In one profound session, an image of a 'tall, native man' wearing a buffalo headdress and animal skins appeared in the corner of the room. I mentioned it.

Ruth said simply. "It's for you."

I sat in awe of this silent vision for almost thirty minutes until it disappeared. What it meant or wanted to tell me wasn't obvious.

That awareness would come later.

MY LIFE IN ADVERTISING CAME to a rather abrupt halt in the early 1990's when the method of retaining directors of commercials with financial guarantees, ceased to be an employment policy with commercial production houses. Admittedly, I was also not very successful as a director plus my stresses were catching up with me. In retrospect, it was a very shallow existence.

I ended up having one significant commercial to direct a few months later. It was created for a well-known television sitcom star who had a reputation for being difficult.

She deserved it, though I now understand that she was dealing with enormous insecurity in contrast to her fame.

THE FIRST DAY OF SHOOTING was fraught with a mistake on my part and a script which she didn't want to do. We clashed in the passive aggressive way for which she was notorious. I approached her the second day stating that I had been with too many people who were dying (AIDS) to be upset over what had happened the day before. I asked if we could start over again and leave Day One behind. To her credit, she agreed.

The script for Day Two was a good fit for her, so we had fun and it went quite well.

Unfortunately, we had a third day of shooting (without her) in which we did pick-up shots. The morning went badly. The agency creative director knew he was about to lose his job, so he tried to make points with the film production company I was working for. Every decision I made, he contradicted. I liken it to trying to walk across a floor covered in rubber cement. You couldn't move forward nor backward without getting stuck.

By lunch we were behind schedule. For the first time in my career, I went home for the hour. I lay on my living-room floor and conversed with Spirit.

I made a deal. If I go back, (it was a very big 'if') and it is a different day on the set, I will leave the film business. But if I go back and it is a repeat of the morning's experience I will stay because it will mean I have more to learn.

I WENT BACK TO THE set. It was an entirely different day. We re-shot the morning footage plus the afternoon's shot list and wrapped up early. I went home, called the production house executives and told them I was quitting.

Their response was “We don’t blame you.” They knew.

I was now unemployed and, as it appeared, I was unemployable. Pain and humiliation can be great teachers as I soon discovered.

RUTH AND ANITA

A FEW YEARS EARLIER, MY therapist, Ruth, had asked me to describe myself. I set about detailing my career. She then asked who I was when I wasn't engaged in that career.

I had no words. How prophetic.

FUMBLING FOR EXPRESSION I CASUALLY mentioned the innate ability I seemed to have in my hands, though I didn't know what to do with it. If I laid my hands on the site of someone's tumour, was I helping the tumour or the body?

Ruth recommended Reiki and one specific teacher, Anita Levin.

A local natural health magazine I opened not five minutes after the session, advertised a course with Anita in just a week or so. I called and booked a personal treatment before the class.

When she laid her hands on me, I felt like I had come home. It was all the confirmation I needed. I was definitely going to be in that class. It completely opened my eyes.

THE COURSE WAS FIRST DEGREE in Reiki from the traditional school but with a focus on emotional release. At the time (1988) there were no books written about Reiki other than one small book of memoirs. The practice wasn't very well known. I absorbed it with a fervor I had never felt in school.

During the class, when my own turn came to get up on a treatment table, there were two others on tables on either side of me. I was nervous about what might happen.

As I was lying there, the woman on my left re-lived being chased and raped by soldiers as a First Nations woman in the early 1800's. I heard her yelping, then the sound of her feet bouncing up and down on the table as she ran, then her muffled screams while being raped.

At the same time, the fellow on the table to my right was silent then suddenly he raised his right arm straight into the air above him as if holding a sword. He stayed in that position for several minutes, and appeared to be engaged in a struggle. Then silence again. The people working on him said his body was ice cold yet he was still breathing. After about twenty minutes, he finally warmed up and shared with Anita that he had been a mercenary on a ship that was engaged in war and sank with him onboard. He was indeed holding up a sword. The time period appeared to be the 1600's.

So, there I was, this pudding lying on a table between them wondering why nothing was happening for me.

But the truth was, I was too terrified to allow it to happen.

WHEN I NEXT SAW RUTH, she asked me how the Reiki course was for me. I told her nothing happened for me on the table. She asked me why I went and I mentioned that I wanted to find out what to do with my hands. She then asked me if I learned that, and I had to agree that I had, in fact, my hands were now on fire.

"It wasn't your time then. You got what you went for."

I had fallen into the trap of comparing my progress to others. It was one good lesson of many more to follow.

I AM MORE THAN GRATEFUL that Anita came into my life. I didn't feel weird for the first time in my life. I had found myself or at least an energetic feeling that felt familiar and loving … at last.

THEN, THROUGH ANITA, I MET Eleanor.

ELEANOR

I TOLD NO-ONE ABOUT MY childhood alien abductee experiences until I was twenty-seven when I told my best friend.

He was speechless. I had clearly made him uncomfortable. Consequently, I clammed up again on that subject until my forties when I was introduced to Eleanor Moore, an extraordinary healer from New Hampshire in the USA.

ELEANOR DIDN'T DO REIKI. SHE just did … Eleanor … and from the age of three. I have never met or heard of anyone like her.

There are many stories about Eleanor. At times I have hesitated to describe her as a human being because so many anomalies happened around her; ice forming on her doorstep in July during a workshop, people spontaneously going into emotional healing upon meeting her, room temperatures nose-diving at workshops only to rise again when that particular round was over, restaurants with subdued clients and staff coming alive when she entered, wait staff unable to keep orders straight, computers and cash registers suddenly and mysteriously malfunctioning. She was known to frequent a store or a snack bar simply to bring healing to someone she knew of there who was in need of it.

Eleanor would refer to it as her 'street work'.

Eleanor's workshops yielded astounding results. People who were insecure, fearful or haunted by their trauma were transformed after one workshop. They were more relaxed, clear and mentally present. It was a privilege to witness these changes.

GO TO WHEREVER YOU ARE CALLED TO GO

ELEANOR USED TO LECTURE ON Carl Jung though she wasn't classically trained in Jungian psychotherapy as I remember. I once asked her where she was travelling to next and she mentioned she was heading to Switzerland (the home of Carl Jung) that following week to do a lecture. Her next words were, "I'm not sure why I have to go. I've done my work already."

This was a clue to her life's work … it manifested outside of linear time.

ELEANOR WOULD LECTURE TO A room that was half full of people seated in chairs. The other half of the room was prepared with yoga mats. Halfway through the lecture the yoga mats would be full of people releasing emotions while the people still in their chairs were bent over holding their heads in their hands.

Eleanor could simply read a booklet of electronic instructions aloud and people would start to release. Her body would set off the metal detectors at airports. Fresh from a workshop, she was once seated between two businessmen on a plane. She asked for ginger ale. As the flight attendant set her drink in front of her, it started to boil. She prayed her seatmates wouldn't notice.

I HAD DECIDED TO STAY over an extra night following a weekend workshop at her farmhouse in the New Hampshire countryside. About 11:00 o'clock as I was getting ready for bed I noticed a very strong light, the intensity of baseball stadium lights, coming from above the roof of the house.

"Wow, talk about overkill yard lights." I thought until I recalled that I had walked around the house exterior earlier in the weekend. There were no lights on the roof at all.

Eleanor then appeared walking down the hallway with towels to put away.

"Eleanor, there are strong lights coming from above the house."

"Oh, it's just a UFO, dear. They've come to talk to me. You'll hear a jet in a few minutes (coming from the Airforce base) then a helicopter. You'd think that after all these years they would ask what was going on."

Exactly as she predicted, a jet made several passes high above the house followed by a helicopter which buzzed us for about forty-five minutes. Then silence.

The lights had vanished.

My childhood had just been ratified. I wasn't crazy after all.

ELEANOR ALWAYS HELD AN INTRODUCTION to her work on the Friday night before a weekend workshop. After a few of these, in which she would re-tell the same stories, I became a bit bored and wanted to skip the Intro night. Anita convinced me that the Intro was very important. So, as my personal form of protest, I arrived a little late to the next one but as I moved along the rows of chairs while

Eleanor was speaking, I became aware that I was moving through alternating shafts of light in gold then silver. The coloured shafts all emanated from Eleanor. I decided to lie on the floor instead of taking a chair. As soon as I closed my eyes, the First Nation's man in the buffalo headdress appeared in my vision once more. The importance of that evening was underscored for me. I never missed or arrived late to another one.

Eleanor's workshops always started with the use of sound. Particular sounds resonated in specific areas of the body. The sound that related to the upper abdomen was a sustained "ahhh." As the session progressed you were able to 'sound' for longer periods of time, often defying any logic. It felt as if the sound could go on for several minutes.

Issues centred in the head could be reached by making a high-pitched "eee" sound. As those sessions progressed, the sound could be expressed at ever higher notes which often felt beyond the range of the person on the table no matter what their normal pitch was.

When you think about it, sound is the only way we can massage and relax the inside of the cranium.

"Ooohhh" resonated in the lower abdomen and could bring up issues around the concept of the self that were held in resistance.

"Hah" repeated rhythmically equated to establishing a sense of self especially in front of authority. A verbal equivalent would be "Who cares what you think!"

Other sounds would be "No" which often raised buried issues of resentment, sexual interference or victimization.

"Yes" repeated rhythmically could affirm a sense of self.

"Ca" was effective with people who often presented the word "can't" in their speech.

Subsequent experimentation on my own revealed that the energy generated by the use of sound could be directed at will.

I would think about my right leg then sound "Yeow!" The energy moved down my right leg to my foot. I could then move it to my left leg with ease by repeating the sound and redirecting my intention.

IN ELEANOR'S WORKSHOPS, WHICH STARTED with everyone sounding, people were spontaneously re-living life as dinosaurs, soldiers who died on the battlefield, or they were screaming and crying over violence several lifetimes ago, but also laughing uncontrollably, singing and tripping through space and time.

Some were also dead silent. It was akin to stepping into an asylum, but it was healing on an extraordinary level.

Initially, in the middle of this chaos, my control issues again felt on the verge of a breach. In the beginning during a break, I felt compelled to ask if anyone had ever seen a person 'lose it' in a session and never get it back. No-one had. I would find myself calmly having tea and cookies with the person who had just relived a past life as a dinosaur minutes earlier. It was intriguing, terrifying and confounding all at the same time.

I REALIZED THAT I NEEDED to come to grips with my fear of losing control. The man who had acted out the dinosaur convinced me. If he could do that in front of everyone, then I could let myself go.

When I finally did, I would find myself flying to other planets, to other lifetimes and to view my histories as a Shaman.

Most importantly, all of my sessions with Eleanor and Anita were suffused with an undeniable sense of safety and love. But, emotional release was critical to my growth and awareness.

It was now time to address my history of suppression.

I was perplexed and curious at the same time. Could all of this emotion and especially the visions be inside my being? I didn't consciously intend to journey to any of the places I ended up in, yet there I was. My world view had just been blown wide open. The fear I had worked so diligently to contain all my life was now available to be understood. I had an outlet which would allow me to examine it and to learn from it with safety.

Eleanor's business card simply read "Energy Consultant."

ALLOW ME TO ATTEMPT AN explanation of what I (we) call 'energy' which differs from the purely scientific definition.

On a physical level, my experience of the 'energy' is more akin to having a subtle, low electric frequency running through my body … a vague buzz or tingling. As it progresses, it can lead to an altered state. Yet, I am not lost because I am still aware of the room I am in, other people and of my breathing. I can perform tasks at will, such as moving my legs, arms, fingers etc. It is a very safe, permissive and loving experience and I am left with a sense of exhilaration and wonder … all by using my breath and sound. Other modalities such as Holotropic Breath Work utilize this altered state. It isn't unique to the work that Anita and Eleanor did, but for me, this advanced state is a very familiar place in Shamanic journeys. It is the place where crystal clear, lucid dreams happen just before I wake in the morning. It is familiar, yet it seems to be beyond linear understanding.

I STRUGGLED WITH HOW TO describe my experience to others. In the early days, I know I was proselytizing like a born-again Fundamentalist but that eventually died down. There were no words that could fully describe what I was feeling and witnessing. I eventually realized that I had to live my own experiences and to allow others to find theirs in time.

LIFE IS AN EXPERIENCE NOT an explanation.

OOKANEE

IN ONE SESSION WITH BOTH Eleanor and Anita, I found myself witnessing a vision of a calm, mirror-like lake bordered by trees yet oddly blue in colour. I then heard the distant sounds of voices repeating, *"Oo ka nee. Oo ka nee."*

I asked Anita if she knew what it might mean.

"Ask," she said.

How simple. So, I asked and the answer that came back was:

"*It's your name, stupid.*"

Okay, I admit that I'm slow on the uptake at times, but what could it mean? Is it obvious to everyone but me?

So many questions now surround my very existence.

ABOUT TWO MONTHS LATER AT my island residence, I walked out onto the front steps late at night. It was mid-week in early Fall, and I was alone. There was no traffic on the lake whatsoever. The stillness pervaded the depth of your being. People who live by lakes know exactly what I am attempting to put into words.

A full moon was rising behind me. I instinctively walked down to the bottom of the front steps and picked up a pine bough that lay there. I was curious as to whether it was full of rust-coloured dead needles or fresh green ones because, in the moonlight, it appeared entirely blue.

I was inspired to dance along the foreshore carving the air with the bough as I moved. This wasn't something I did at all, but the dance moved distinctly and undeniably through me.

When I finally stopped, I mounted the steps again, turned and looked out at the lake and sang out,

"Oo kan ee!"

"What does that mean?" I mused and then it struck me.

There in front of me was the vison I had months ago. My name means "Dances in full moon by still water."

I make no claim to First Nations' heritage, yet it was coming to me spontaneously.

SHAMANISM

IN 1988, JUST AFTER MY first course in Reiki with Anita, I was encouraged by my friend Rolf Erdmann to take a course in Shamanism. Michael Harner's Institute ran the course in Toronto. I decided to sign up. It was interesting and strangely familiar but what really intrigued me was a follow-up course offered by Sandra Ingerman on Death and Dying. You would have thought I had enough of the subject after living in the middle of the worst of the AIDS crisis. I lost several very close friends and many acquaintances. What intrigued me though, was the experience of the spirit after death.

In one specific journey, Sandra mentioned that we would next explore where we go after we die. She then gave instructions on how to proceed there. I had an amazing journey that exceeded my expectations. Then I heard her say "Now wait for the drum."

Huh? My initial feelings were that I had messed up, but when I reflected on it, I had accomplished the entire journey in the space of her first three words while she was still explaining the procedure. My whole journey had transpired in mere seconds but felt much, much, longer and complete.

I was immediately aware that the white noise in my head that I had been so determined to shut down for my whole life was in fact a lightning-fast shamanic journey space. I recognized that it had been with me since childhood but in my need to appear normal, I shut it down. It also occurred to me that this was a portal outside of linear time.

This too, was the space I experienced when I would 'daydream'. I had journeyed shamanically throughout my life.

I distinguish this 'noise' from the tapes my brain plays and re-plays that are based upon negative life trauma and experiences. Those nagging 'voices' or tapes are not actually me … I am the person who is listening. But I had somehow allowed them to permeate my unconscious and given them free rein over my sense of self. I have since discovered that it is my responsibility to silence those tapes.

What works best for me, forgive my language here, is to yell "Shut the fuck up!" in my mind or even out loud.

It seems harsh, but believe me it works. For me that phrase is an absolute expletive. As a command, it's a brick wall. It may require repeating a few times but it's worth it.

HEALING SESSIONS WITH ELEANOR AND ANITA, 1990

MANY OF THE SESSIONS I experienced with Anita and Eleanor were profound and at the same time confusing. I would find myself piloting a space craft similar to one depicted in Star Wars. The body of the craft was filled with seats as found in a large, commercial aircraft. Every seat was occupied by people I didn't know, yet somehow, I felt responsible for them. We were flying out into the universe then right into one specific planet that I sensed may be Mars. As we passed over the surface of the planet a wide cave-like opening appeared and we flew into it. What was revealed was a world not unlike Earth but with its own sky, land mass and sea. After the session ended I mused about whether or not my Ego had been playing tricks on me, but that didn't feel correct. Another session took me to a planet where large "buildings" appeared to be made of or held together with transparent energy. The buildings felt to me that they were great halls of higher learning and that I was there for some purpose. The surface of the "walls" reminded me of the coloured effect that oil reflects when mixed with water. People were moving about on raised pathways also held together with energy. Why I was there wasn't clear, but I definitely had the sense that I was supposed to be there.

In another session I found myself in complete darkness. As my 'eyes' became accustomed to the absence of light, I was able to discern a vague image of a wooden post rising up behind my right shoulder. An oppressive weight was bearing down upon my whole body, yet I could still 'breathe'.

As my eyes became further accustomed to the lack of light, at Anita's suggestion, I looked down at my body. It was a very dried up structure of brown-stained bones, long strands of hair and what appeared to be rawhide. At the same time, I heard distant voices chanting, almost in sotte voce. Their words became louder until I made out what they were saying,

"*Come back, you must come back.*"

The voices persisted, getting louder with every repetition.

Finally, I had to acknowledge that they were speaking … about and to me. I decided to appeal to reason by saying,

"I can't come back; I am exhausted and have no strength."

I immediately found myself standing outside what appeared to be the mound in which I had been buried, thus the sense of weight.

Then, out of the sky a large shaft of bright, white, translucent light appeared that enveloped me completely. I started to float upwards within it. The voices continued.

A similarly translucent image of a turtle appeared outside the shaft of light. As I rose upwards, it accompanied me, moving outside the shaft then inside of me. At the time, I had no idea what the significance of this could be.

I rose above the clouds and ended up standing upon one particular cloud. The multiple voices became one pervasive male voice repeating those words once again to me, "*Come back. You must come back.*"

I was becoming irritated by the insistence and decided to appeal to reason once more.

"I can't come back, just look at my body." I replied.

Immediately there was a flash of light around me. I was given the body of a young native man dressed in rawhide.

I expressed my frustration, "Why should I come back? They didn't listen to me before."

The voice then said, "*They have no choice. They have to listen now.*"

Realizing that I was the one who clearly had no choice, I angrily shot back, pointing my finger as I spoke, "Okay, I'll come back but it's the LAST time I ever come back!"

"*All-right.*" The voice said.

Then I demanded, still ticked, "Now what will I have to help me?"

In my right hand a stick appeared. It had a ball on the end with things inside of it. A belt appeared at my waist with a small, beaded pouch.

The vision ended.

WHAT DIDN'T THEY LISTEN TO before? What will compel them to listen now? And who are 'they'? Will I remember what it was about? Further, what meaning, what role and most importantly what responsibility did this portend for my life?

I noted that the voices were not saying, "Go back, you must go back," rather "Come back, you must come back." The voices were clearly attached to the earth and my existence there, not the spirit realm as I knew it.

I had a strong sense that my life was about to make a sharp turn.

THE DAY AFTER HARNER'S COURSE on Shamanism, I stopped into a shop called Skin and Bones run by a First Nations man. My plan was to buy a drum and a rattle. I spent about two hours going through the native-made drums to find the one that spoke in resonance with my heart's voice. After about two hours, I settled on one, purchased it and left.

I returned the next day to look for a rattle but the young man who was serving me never quite got what I was looking for. I was about to depart when the owner of the shop left people he was serving, walked around behind the counters and up to where the young man was standing. He then bent down and pulled out a rattle that was clearly hidden from view.

"This is the rattle he is looking for." He said to the young man.

He looked directly at me. It was a four-directions rattle, a match to the "stick with a ball on it" from my vision.

He knew.

In retrospect I realized that perhaps unconsciously, Rolf also 'knew' and had directed me to Michael Harner's Course.

Shortly thereafter, a friend gifted me a beautiful medicine pouch that she had beaded herself. My tools had arrived.

I MAKE A POINT OF stating in my courses that I do not teach First Nation's Shamanism, but rather I teach how to access a universal state termed Shamanism that I feel strongly is the birthright of all human beings. Shamanism, as a calling within me, always manifested feelings of "Imposter Syndrome" until I fully embraced the constant stream of messages and experiences that surrounded me almost daily. I could no longer ignore them.

Harner's Institute refers to this as Core Shamanism.

I refer to it as Innate Shamanism.

THE POWER OF STORIES

STORYING IS ONE OF THE many things I learned from Eleanor and Anita. That knowledge was furthered by witnessing a Haida speaker. She had come to Toronto on behalf of the elders in the 1990's warning we only had six years left in which to turn back the tide of climate change. The lecture took place in a very large lecture hall with raked seating.

As she spoke, she took long pauses between the thoughts she expressed. I sat there and felt a wave of energy moving upwards through the hall in the silence after each sentence. At one point I thought I would be blown out of my seat by the force of the energy unleashed by the import of her statements.

It underscored for me the importance of speaking truth, selecting the right words then leaving pauses so that people could fully absorb what had just been spoken.

That experience changed how I spoke and listened … forever.

AT A SMALL RECEPTION AFTER her speech, I felt compelled to share with her a brief version of the vision of 'Coming back'.

Her answer was short and succinct.

"The Elders are moving through many people now."

I then realized who was speaking to me when I heard "*Come back. You must come back.*" The land where Native elders are buried is sacred. They are still there. It is their 'heaven'.

TWO YEARS LATER, I WENT to Haida Gwaii to participate in a kayak trip. Haida Gwaii, is the ancestral home of the Haida Nation. My travel companion and I were guests of Kevin and Katie Borserio while we were there. Kevin had arranged the kayak trip for us.

Shortly after we arrived, Kevin received a call that engaged him for almost half an hour, When the call ended, Katie asked him what happened. The Haida mentor he was close to had lost her footing while gathering sea urchins and inadvertently placed her hand down onto the spines of a sea urchin. Her hand had become so badly infected, she had to be taken to a hospital on the mainland and put on antibiotics ... but it hadn't helped. She was obviously in great pain. Kevin said that he had never heard her cry.

When I heard this, I mulled over whether it was appropriate of me to offer her healing when I was clearly in her medicine area not my own.

But she agreed to the assistance. The swelling and redness reduced in her hand to a near normal state. I told her that I would send her healing while I was on the kayak trip.

We had plenty of time between kayak locations to send healing.

It occurred to me as I was sending her healing to ask her if she knew the Haida speaker I met back in Toronto but whose name had now escaped my memory. Haida speakers must be aware of each other, I assumed. As I was about to send her healing, it occurred to me that she was, in fact, that person.

What are the chances of that?

When we returned, Kevin told me that the woman, whose name is Diane Brown, had asked to see me again. When I saw her. I asked if she had spoken in Toronto on behalf of the elders a few years ago. She had. Thus became the opportunity to convey to her how hearing her speak had completely re-focused the way I spoke and listened.

I expressed my gratitude. It was no coincidence.

As I was about to leave, she gave me a jar of salmon and an eagle feather, which I recognized was a sacred gift. Two other people had previously offered to give me an eagle feather, but it didn't feel right, so I declined. Diane was obviously the right person.

That feather is still with me over thirty years later.

KEVIN AND KATIE TOOK US to their magical driftwood cabin, on a beach quite a distance north after the kayak trip. On the way there, Kevin admitted to me that he had experienced problems with his left knee, left testicle, his left hip and shoulder. Refer to the diagrams at the end of the chapter *Notting Hill Gate, London, 1968* for references to the possible issue that may have been located there. Kevin was in excellent physical condition, so it wasn't a matter of age and deterioration.

I offered to work with him at the cabin which he readily accepted.

We set up a table in a back room. I scanned his body about a foot above it so that I would know where his body needed me to start. After a few minutes of simply laying my hands on him, Kevin's face was knotted in a tight grimace. He had entered the emotional experience that held his knee, testicle, hips and shoulder in painful resistance. After forty minutes or so of this, I asked him what he was experiencing and where he was.

"I'm half salmon and half eagle and I can't get out of the water."

The session ended abruptly about ten minutes later when he sat up and ran out the door to his truck with me right behind him. We drove about fifteen minutes away to a phone booth (this was pre-cell phones). He had to contact Diane. The phone call lasted for about thirty-five minutes.

When he returned to the truck he said "She bathed me in Haida … and welcomed me home."

"We've been waiting for you." she said.

The larger story here is that Kevin had been a teacher at the local high school and was seconded by Diane Brown, an elder and a community leader, to teach Haida to the community.

Diane realized that the numbers of native speakers were declining on Haida Gwaii. An alphabet had already been created because there are sounds for which there are no English equivalents. Kevin had drawn Haida speaking elders into the class to teach the Haida culture, crafts and language. He then gave them high school credits in exchange for their participation. The elders couldn't wait to return to school in the Fall.

Diane and her family had adopted Kevin, Katie and their family as Haida so that he could teach their language as a Haida … a very high honour.

However, he didn't feel that he deserved to teach the language as a white person inside their community.

That changed for him after our session and his subsequent call to Diane. It was soon revealed to me that she and her family are members of the Eagle clan. White people were often referred to as salmon.

It wasn't lost on me that Diane had gifted me an eagle feather and a jar of salmon.

The translation of Kevin's physical symptoms and their meaning for me was as follows: knee represents inflexibility or indecision, left testicle represents a perceived lack of empowerment in his upbringing or environment, left hip related to his sense of self and his environment, and left shoulder suggests a conflict with the responsibility expected of him.

The understanding and relevance came from him in his session.

Unfortunately, Diane's hand did not heal completely and continued to be a chronic problem for her for a few years.

I DON'T READ MANY BOOKS, very few in fact. I have learned to be cautious about allowing someone else's truth to pollute my own experiences. However, one book that had a great positive influence on my journey was *Rolling Thunder* by Doug Boyd.

Rolling Thunder, by then a medicine man in the Shoshone Nation, could summon the weather, and in one incident, a tornado.

Something in me knew I could also summon the weather and on the occasions when it felt absolutely critical, it worked. I have learned that I can speak to the Weather Spirits directly as I will describe later, but I have full respect for that force of nature moving about our planet with an intelligence that is awe inspiring.

Rolling Thunder also introduced me to an awareness of bees and medicinal plants. I cannot recommend the book highly enough.

THE GIFT OF FEAR

IN THE EARLY 1980's WHEN the tsunami of AIDS appeared on the horizon of my awareness, I was once again almost crippled by fear. Initially, people were dying within three days of a diagnosis.

It appeared to be unstoppable and incurable. It was not met with any official responses that it existed other than feeble political recognition. We were alone in that fight for survival.

I was managing to suppress my brimming fear while in a high-stress work environment but occasionally it would spill out, usually over a sense of failure or criticism … my Achilles heel.

I suspect it also had a lot to do with suppressed and deeply internalized feelings of religious guilt such as God punishing me for being a homosexual.

Then a woman, with whom I worked, spoke the wisest words I heard throughout the entire epidemic.

"You know, Bernie, there are two things out there. There is AIDS and then there is the fear of AIDS, and I'm not sure which is more fatal."

I felt that I had been hit by lightning.

I LEFT HER OFFICE AND went straight home. I was determined not to let Fear own me. I lay on my living-room floor and wrestled this entity called 'Fear' out of my body. It took over two hours but when I finished, the carpet was soaked with sweat beneath me.

I was never afraid of AIDS again.

I adopted the acronym for AIDS which was Accelerated Inner Development Syndrome. For me, that … is what it was.

But … the gift that fear offers is this. If you are willing to go into the fear, to really examine it, to take it to an understanding of what actually triggers it (death, humiliation, violence, lack of safety, abandonment) … you will encounter extraordinary growth.

IT WAS DURING THIS CHAOTIC period that I was introduced to Louise Hay's work. To my surprise, we had identical descriptions for several of the observations of the body I had arrived upon some twenty years earlier in England.

It appeared that I had hit on some universal truths after all.

BECAUSE I WASN'T AN AVID reader, I had missed the reported early warning signs about AIDS posted in *The Village Voice* by Larry Kramer, in particular. A good friend of mine, Scott Cline, was completely plugged in, however, and sounded the alarm to me. This was in the free-wheeling days of uninhibited sexual hook-ups. I noticed that I had developed an internal sense of who was and who was not a safe sexual partner. It turned out that I was never wrong. When I sat with the character of this awareness, I questioned whether the knowledge came from within me, outside of me, the energy around people, or from a higher source. It would always start as a felt sense, a gut feeling, then move up into my consciousness. I came to understand that I was being informed internally where the danger for me existed. I started to listen more intently to my innate response.

Any time I went against that feeling in my life, I regretted it.

IN SPITE OF HIS EXTENSIVE research and his sense of responsibility to the community, it was already too late for Scott. His death was a very big loss for many of us.

HENRY

I HAD NEVER BEEN PARTICULARLY adept nor appropriate around the issue of dating. I honestly felt too weird to allow anyone in to see the truth of my being. I was easily swept off my stability and often became inappropriately needy if anyone showed interest in me. A chance encounter changed all of that.

HENRY ARRIVED AT THE ISLAND as a guest of the person I was currently attempting to date. Both my date and Henry's were doomed from the start but a few months later, it was suggested by one of them that Henry and I would make a good couple. After a few moments of reflection, I realized that we could at least enjoy art galleries together. He was an artist, a musician and a teacher. When I conjure up my experience of him on that first meeting at the Island, there was a light, much like a halo around his head.

Having missed the start time of the movie we had planned to see, our first date over lunch then turned into watching The Santa Claus parade down University Avenue in Toronto. I caught a sideways glimpse of him watching the marching bands and knew instantly that this would be a long-term relationship for us both.

He was extraordinary. As our relationship progressed and deepened I began to trust him with any part of my life, no matter how weird I felt saying it. I had found my life's soul mate. I was no longer alone.

He had been rejected by his parents when it was revealed that he was gay. They subsequently did not speak to him, nor he to them, for six years. In spite of this, I recognized the deep love he had for his parents and encouraged him with the assistance of his siblings to reconnect. Henry had also just been diagnosed with AIDS so I felt it was important to address any negativity I could around him. We had been together a year and a half.

For me, his diagnosis was a body blow that I had to ignore.

In order to allow him the freedom to flourish in the time he had left, my sorrow and sense of betrayal by Spirit had to be contained at all costs. I lost a sense of compassion in so doing. I am not proud of some of my actions then, but it was all I could muster in the moment. The carpet of expectation and love was about to be wrenched from the ground beneath me. Fear loomed up silently, my own Loch Ness monster, but I would have to deal with it later.

Meanwhile, Henry personally embraced Eleanor and Anita's workshops. He participated willingly. Anything that afforded any possibility of healing he would throw himself into. Many times, I would come home to the acrid smell of Chinese herbs being boiled for an elixir. They tasted as bad as they smelled but Henry would down them like fresh spring water.

His impending exit loomed over all of my thoughts the last few years. The loss I feared was overwhelming. Yet, I didn't feel that I could burden him with my own sense of hopelessness.

Was that a fear I needed to face head on? I am still not sure whether that was the wisest course of action. My very existence was floating on an unfathomable vortex of unexpressed grief.

NONETHELESS, THROUGH HENRY I WAS catapulted into a high level of spiritual growth. He had encouraged me like no-one else had and it was he who identified the moving passion within me for the work I now do. His life on both sides of the veil has been a gift to my soul … but more about that later.

FEAR AND ECUADOR

IN 1995, A YEAR AFTER Henry passed, I joined an excursion along with two friends to visit Shamen in the rain and cloud forests of Ecuador. The entire trip is itself a story but what I wish to relay is yet another example of facing fear. In a remote Shuar village, a camp for tourists had been erected near a river but in dense Amazonian jungle. To give you an idea of how remote this camp was, it would help to know that the Shuar were headhunters only about twenty years earlier. The most common cause of death was from snakes. Pathways were cleared of brush back five feet or more on either side so that snakes could be readily seen and avoided. All visitors had to wear high rubber boots.

Children would walk up to two days through the jungle to attend the school there. What most impressed me about the schooling was that in the second grade, they taught students how to teach. The children were encouraged to learn how to teach the students in the grade below them. It is a great system.

The river nearby is isolated in a deep gorge as it moves past the village. The only access was across a suspension bridge with wooden planks but with no guide ropes to hold onto. As you walked across, the bridge would start to undulate up and down with the movements of your footsteps. It was quite unnerving. Jane, one of my friends on the trip is the bravest person I know. She just forged directly across then reminded me not to look down as we traversed. She was right. I had a fear of heights. By the second day we were tramping across that bridge four at a time without breaking step. It was exhilarating.

The path across the bridge led to a more accessible section of the river with two pond-like open areas. We were instructed not to swim in the upper pond but the lower one was clear for our use. The reason we were cautioned not to use the upper pond is because that was the snake's pond, anacondas to be exact. The phrase "When in Rome, do as the Romans do." sprang into my mind. I entered the water and waded across to a rock in the centre. I could feel anacondas slithering past my legs, more than likely out of curiosity.

The whole time I was in the water I kept reminding myself that I was not in their pond and therefore under the laws of the Shuar, I was safe.

Then, that evening two medical doctors and their wives arrived at the camp along with a few other guests. They had come up the Amazon from Brazil where they were attending a conference.

Over dinner, the wife of one of the doctors asked us what we did, presumably for a living. Two of us answered that we were spiritual healers. You could practically hear the social dialogue door slam shut as she turned to speak to someone else. Her husband subsequently acted quite haughtily towards us. I wondered why he had come. But I recognized that he too had to cross the bridge and bathe in the pond.

As I suspected, he was terrified. He crawled across the bridge on his hands and knees accompanied by two men. Then it took the same two men to lower him into the water to bathe. He could barely suppress his hysteria.

His nose was much closer to the earth after that, though he never did speak to us. However, the other doctor in their group couldn't have been more open, kind and curious about indigenous Shamanism and the spiritual culture.

FACING ANOTHER FEAR

I HAD BEEN SPEAKING TO two friends of mine at Stony Lake late one afternoon. The woman, Sunny Cook, was a special friend with whom, as we discovered, I shared a history in Reiki with Anita Levin. Sunny had been a big supporter of my work. The other person was Rolf Erdmann, the close friend who had encouraged me to investigate Shamanism

On a good night, Rolf would cycle around the lake to an isolated spot, hide his bicycle in the bushes then tramp through the woods, throw his sleeping bag on the ground and fall asleep.

Once a year, Sunny would go on a self-imposed fast for three days alone in the woods with only a hatchet and some water. She would construct a lean-to then settle into meditation. My reaction was to ask her if bears ever came around.

"Oh, they do!" she said. "They push on the door."

"How do you handle that?" I asked.

"Oh, I just pray harder." She said calmly.

"I could never do that." I admitted to them both. "I'm afraid of bears."

They looked at me and said in unison, "Then you have to do it!"

They were right. I had no choice but to face it.

A WEEK LATER I ARRANGED to borrow Rolf's kayak and a tent for my first kayak trip. I telephoned my parents to tell them I would be away for a few days.

"You're doing what?" my Father said.

I was no longer an adult of forty-two years old but had somehow regressed to the age of a naive twelve-year old.

"Have you ever done this before?" he then said.

"Does anyone know where you're going?"

I assured him that Rolf knew where I was going.

"So, you're going on this trip, alone for the first time …"

I could hear him suppressing the words "Have you lost your God damned mind?"

"Are you taking a gun? he then said.

"No, thanks, I won't need one."

"How about a hatchet?" he offered, still appalled at my decision.

I agreed to take the hatchet in order to soothe his anxiety.

So … I came by my fear naturally it seems … my parents were vibrating with it. It wasn't mine.

After a few more exchanges on the topic, I lost my reserve and stated that if anything happened to me on the trip I would hold them responsible. They, after all, were holding out fearful thoughts for my safety.

"Think warm, positive, safe thoughts, please."

The conversation ended.

IT WAS THE END OF September. I was alone on Bark Lake.

I had taken all the precautions with my food and had strung it high in the air between two trees. The week sped by at an unconscious rate. As I settled in for my last night, I pondered about the week and my intention … which was to confront my fear of bears. Yet, I had seen no sign of one at all.

No sooner had that thought crossed my mind when I heard a bawling animal calling across the water. I froze.

Then my rational brain kicked in. I'm on an island and that animal, which admittedly sounded like a bear, was on the mainland about a half a kilometer away. I relaxed.

Then I heard a splash.

Again, my brain assured me that there was considerable distance between us. But about ten minutes later I heard an animal exit the lake very close to me. I heard the water dripping off its body.

Anxiety crept up and into my throat. This was it … the purpose of my whole trip. I decided to face my fear and unzipped my tent flap so that a screen was all that separated me from the bear.

I waited.

THE MORNING SUN WARMING MY face woke me. It was about seven o'clock. I had slept soundly. I was both surprised and honestly … disappointed.

THEN TEN MONTHS LATER, I travelled to Red Mountain, B.C. for a further course in Reiki, this time Mastery.

We had to bring our own tents. Campsites had recently been plowed so that we had level, designated sites. We were warned that there were bears around and not to bring food of any sort into our tents, not even toothpaste.

As I lay there waiting to fall asleep, I mused about how I would react if a bear appeared. At that precise moment I realized that my back was very warm, almost hot. I turned over to see if that would happen to my front. In fact, the wall of the tent was quite hot. It took me a few seconds to realize that a bear or some large animal must be on the other side of that thin, nylon tent.

It's body heat was emanating right through the tent wall.

MY NEXT MEMORY IS OF waking up. It was morning. I had fallen asleep enveloped in the warmth radiating through the wall of the tent. My skeptical brain wasn't reassured that this might have been a bear until I checked outside the tent. Next to the wall was a large indentation the size of a bear. Bear paw prints surrounded my tent. The whole incident hadn't triggered anxiety at all, conversely, I was strangely comforted by it.

It was all the confirmation I needed. My body knew I was safe.

Fear can be a mighty great teacher.

Example

I have worked with many clients who had difficulty coping with fear. When we were able to delve into the source of the fear, it often turned out that they were raised with an underlying fear handed to them by their parents or older siblings. It wasn't theirs.

One woman in a session kept repeating,

"It didn't happen, it didn't happen, it didn't happen." For several minutes.

"What didn't happen?" I finally asked.

"Sexual abuse." She answered.

Yet she had no memory of it.

At the end of the day, I cautioned the students not to share anything that had happened because we still had another day to complete. Often the context and conclusion for the first session came on the second day.

But that first evening she shared the content of that initial session with her parents. The next morning I received frantic calls from her parents denying that there was ever sexual abuse in the family. It eventually came out that both her parents had been sexually abused as children and had never spoken to each other about it. My client, in fact, had not been abused but the suppressed fear of her parents was transferred to her as a child.

THE BODY KNOWS

WHEN YOU CONSIDER IT, MOST often a flash of fear doesn't start in your head but in your body, most likely in your gut or even your legs and knees.

The first time I became fully aware that this "intelligence" existed beyond my brain, I was driving a few people to a political event. I thought I saw a large piece of what appeared to be blue construction tarp being blown through the air by the wind and onto the street to the left of me. As my mind was trying to make sense of what it was, a person sitting in the back seat exclaimed that a young boy had just been hit by a car in the other lane.

Yet the image had appeared in slow-motion to me. What was even more fascinating to me was that my foot was already on the brake and my hands were fully engaged in gripping the steering wheel. In fact, I was already in the process of pulling over when my brain caught up and recognized that the object flying in slow-motion was indeed a young boy.

He was unhurt, I am happy to say.

The point of this story is that my body already knew how to respond. My brain or consciousness was a few seconds behind.

So how did my body know? Why did the whole incident appear in slow motion? Is this instinct connected to my eyes before it informs my conscious? How does it see? Is there a version of myself that exists beyond my body that has hyper-awareness? Can I access that intelligence at will?

Further, what is the nature of that intelligence? Is it connected to my instinct, to my subconscious or are they one and the same.

IN THE EARLY 1990's THIS intelligence smacked me right upside the head.

THE DARK SIDE

I HAD BEEN VOCAL AND critical of someone in a nearby town who had taken a weekend course in Reiki. All levels of Reiki, First Degree, Second Degree and Mastery were accorded in that one weekend. The training I was affiliated with required at least two months between First and Second Degrees and at least two years to reach the level of Mastery. What bothered me most was the dishonouring of the teachings which I considered sacred. Reiki as a practice and a teaching appeared to become more and more diluted as the years ensued.

In my next class, I made the mistake of mentioning my disappointment. That information made its way back to the person in question.

What followed was a war.

A FEW WEEKS LATER, I discovered that I had been targeted by a coven of "witches" that was created by this person for the sole purpose of eliminating me either physically, making me quite ill or at least re-locating me out of the area. I knew this because a few former students of mine had inadvertently been approached to join that circle.

I HADN'T BEEN FEELING WELL lately, almost dizzy and at times couldn't think clearly. Also, the requests for my teaching were diminishing quite noticeably.

The next day, as I drove back from town I struggled with what, if anything, to do to counter this offensive. I noticed lights flashing at a distance ahead. At the same time, I felt myself moving into an altered state.

I was being sent a message and I could feel it.

Right in the middle of the intersection where two rural roads converged with clear views in all directions, and positioned precisely in the centre, was a horse that appeared to be dead and had been hit by a car. The horse's legs were extended as if it were a statue that had been knocked over. There were no apparent injuries. The car that hit it was off to my right side and I noticed that it was light blue in colour. There were also two police cars with lights flashing. One policeman gestured to me to go around this scene. As I continued past the accident along the road, I started to come out of the altered state.

The whole incident was a signal for me.

Although this is a rural area, there were no horses in the farms in that vicinity. I have since asked if anyone had ever seen horses in that area … to this day no-one ever has.

It was definitely a message.

The symbolic meaning came to me as follows. I had just been thinking about what to do about the situation of the coven when this altered state enveloped me. The horse for me is a symbol of strength but reversed it's a symbol of weakness. It was located in the absolute centre of the intersection of two roads heading in different directions. The car was blue, the colour of the throat chakra, the energy centre of speech. Two symbols of authority were warning of danger and to move around this issue.

It was very clear to me. I had to be silent. I decided to drop any further mention of this person ... but the attacks were just beginning.

The point of the story is that there was wisdom or precognition in this altered state. Or, perhaps my own wisdom was somehow more accessible in this state because my linear mode of thinking was put to one side. Nonetheless, the wisdom was undeniable.

What followed over the next two plus years was volley after volley of psychic attacks. For me, this situation was a very valuable teaching in how to protect oneself from the negative and malevolent intentions of others no matter how intense those efforts are. I am so much stronger as a result of that whole experience, as seriously endangering as it became.

In the end, all paths are equal. Everyone proceeds on their journey at their own pace, by their own standards. I simply had to learn to trust the process of my own journey. Lesson learned.

BY 2004, I HAD STARTED to separate myself from teaching Reiki. The organization I supported had become bound by standardized rules and definitions. Reiki originated as the result of a mystical experience that occurred to Mikao Usui many decades ago. Yet, I referred to Reiki as spiritual healing for which I received criticism. My experiences didn't fit the evolution of the formal teaching. I always taught my students not to simply do Reiki, but to become

Reiki. Let it speak through everything you do. I also taught that it could change your life for which I received further criticism, yet every student I have taught would confirm that statement.

Consequently, I left Reiki formally, but it was and still is a big part of who I am. In truth, teaching Reiki often felt like I was mining the same old scripts. It was time to explore my own growth.

ALLOW THE ANIMAL SPIRITS TO LEAD YOU

WHEN MY PARTNER, HENRY, PASSED over in 1994, the animal spirits took care of me.

He had been hospitalized once again. It looked like his death was imminent, but he had been there before and walked away. All of his vital signs had normalized during the day so the hypervigilance I felt could relax a bit. His family had all arrived at the hospital from out of town, and wanting to allow them privacy I decided to go out for a meal with some of the friends who had gathered. As we were leaving the parking lot, a crow was standing two feet from my side of the car looking directly at me. I noticed it and thought it unusual. I was curious if this was a message.

THAT NIGHT, I CHOSE TO stay in a suite reserved for this occasion in the hospital. I was exhausted. As I left to go to bed, I asked the nursing station to wake me if there were any change in him at all.

At about 3:00 am I heard a crow calling from the ledge outside the window of the room I was in. In my semi-sleep state, I mused about the fact that crows aren't active at night and they certainly don't make noise because a predatory owl could then locate them. Just then, I heard a knock at the door and a nurse told me Henry had passed away.

A friend told me that his spirit had come to her that night even though they had never met. He appeared at the end of her bed and she simply asked who he was.

"*I'm Henry,*" he said.

"Oh, hello Henry. How can I help you?"

"*I want someone to take care of Bernie,*" he said.

"I will do that." she answered. Then as quickly as he had appeared, he left.

THINK ABOUT IT. HE HADN'T met her in this life yet his spirit knew not only where to find her but he also recognized who she was.

As I waited for his family to arrive at the hospital, I took his possessions from the room to my vehicle. There on the roof of the wing Henry was in, was a crow cawing loudly as if announcing an important event. It was still barely morning.

Later in the morning, when I arrived at the marina parking lot, right there sitting on the fence that delineated our parking spaces, a crow was waiting for me. Then as I was walking up to our island residence from the boathouse, I looked around and a crow was walking up the pathway right behind me.

In the midst of the emotional turmoil, I felt strangely comforted.

AFTER HIS DEATH, I WENT on retreat … a kayak trip to Lake Superior initially with Rolf and his partner then by myself for a week.

I was looking for a place to ritualize my grief and to assist Henry's spirit to move on. After paddling for quite a while, I was about to give up and turn back to a site I knew. Just as I had that thought, a gull flew low over my head from behind me.

It flew ahead of me a few hundred meters and turned sharply right.

"Okay," I thought. "That's the spot."

It was. The bank was covered in fragrant herbs. The perfume was intoxicating. I was able to pitch my tent safely on a bank in the herb meadow. It was a gift to my senses.

ON YET ANOTHER KAYAK TRIP, this time to the North Shore of Lake Huron, I had camped on an island with a full view of the lake westward. On my third day there, when I awoke, the sky had grown dark and foreboding. A wind was building. A storm felt imminent and could last a few days. I decided to decamp, load up my kayak and head back to my departure site at the harbour outside of the town of Spanish. Because there was now a strong wind coming off the lake, I took a route that was protected by a series of small islands on both sides of me. I passed a colony of gulls who had claimed one small island as their own. Unusually, they weren't fussed by my presence in their territory though I passed by quite close to them. I then arrived at a long stretch of water that was not protected by islands on the final reach toward Spanish. I had just gotten started when the wind started to gust quite fiercely. Waves were suddenly rising up more than three meters (six plus feet). The troughs between the waves were shorter than the length of my kayak, which meant I couldn't change direction or go back. I was now forced to follow the waves to a rocky inhospitable shoreline or out onto the wide expanse of Lake Huron — if I could manage to crest a wave. Then, the waves started to break as they rose up on my left. Swamping, or worse yet, overturning my loaded kayak was a real possibility. I sensed I was in grave danger and could die out there unobserved by anyone who might offer assistance. Significantly, I wasn't at all afraid.

I spoke to Spirit, "*I could die today and that would be okay with me, but I think I have more work to do. If you agree, I need your assistance to find a way out of this.*"

Within seconds a small formation of three gulls swooped over my head from behind. Flying low just ahead, they showed me the s-shaped passageway and the rhythm around the waves I needed to adopt to negotiate my passage successfully. I did exactly as I was shown. The gulls departed. I paddled rigorously and quickly made my way across the reach.

I HAVE NEVER LOOKED AT gulls again without remembering that teaching and giving thanks. They are guides and pathfinders.

I promised myself to keep that agreement with Spirit for the rest of my life.

AT SIGNIFICANT TIMES, ANIMAL MESSENGERS often appear. Wolves would run across the road in front of me, even on busy highways, and kept reminding me that I was supposed to be a teacher.

At the lake where I lived in summer, my neighbour and close friend Meg died quite unexpectedly in an automobile accident. Rolf, who helped care for her place, and I were sitting on the deck of her cottage shortly after her death. We were talking about her when a hummingbird buzzed both of us, at eye level right in front of our faces. It retreated to a tree three feet away then buzzed us again. I asked Rolf if he had ever seen a bird do that. He hadn't. Neither had I. We looked at each other and said in unison,

"It's Meg."

She was right there with us.

WHAT HAPPENS WHEN WE DIE? WHERE DO WE GO?

THIS OFTEN COMES UP. I personally don't have a formal religion-based belief. What is relevant for me when working with the dying is the belief of the person who passes, but even then, there are anomalies.

A GREAT MAN WHOM I admired when I lived in Newfoundland, did not believe in an afterlife. He was very clear about it.

"You die and that's it." He often said.

"We'll see." I remembered thinking.

After he passed, I decided to check in with him.

"*Well, I didn't know this would happen!*" He blurted out.

He was very agitated, so I worked at calming him

I told him how he could now visit anyone he desired by simply intending to. I also mentioned that he was no longer limited by solid structures such as walls. Surprisingly, he was open to my suggestions but did not question my presence on that side.

He and his wife were very close. She passed over recently and they are together again.

Unconsciously, it was his version of Heaven … it was hers too.

I wondered if everyone who doesn't believe in an afterlife had the same experience. Others with whom I have checked ended up in their personal version of 'Heaven' which may be a garden, a lake, a woods, or glen, on a cloud next to their God … it differs widely and is unique to each person.

People on this side want immediate proof that their loved ones are still around and become saddened when it doesn't happen quickly. But there is no linear time on that side, so what may seem like an eternity on this side is but a millisecond there.

Communication can be by a familiar smell or taste, a sense of being touched, a memory or an incident.

Example: Henry Hassen

After Henry passed, I felt him around me for years. Friends thought I was holding onto him, but it wasn't me. He had full permission to move on and I made sure he knew, but he elected to stay around me … and he painted the most spectacular sunsets that year.

As an example, after he passed, I often had trouble locating my car keys. For the record, I have very specific key habits. They are usually in one of two places without fail. However, after Henry's death I would lose them … constantly.

After wasting considerable time searching, they would appear right where I last placed them. I became suspicious. I asked the other island house members if they were losing things that they were sure they remembered placing. They all confirmed my suspicion. Henry loved attention and he was playing games with us. Thereafter I would 'yell' at him if the game went on too long. Whatever was lost reappeared without fail and right where I knew I had left it.

One instance stands out. The piano in the island residence was a 1908 Heintzman grand piano with legs that were carved into owls. It was magnificent but badly in need of tuning and repair.

We were hosting a wedding, so I decided to have it tuned.

The piano tuner gave me a quote and told me it shouldn't take more than an hour or so. Two and a half hours later, I checked in on him. He was clearly frustrated.

"Pianos usually want me to tune them." He said,

"But this one has been fighting me no matter what I try to do. The keyboard became jammed when I attempted to remove it. Everything resists me, but don't worry, I won't charge you more than I quoted."

I absorbed this and walked out of the room. Then it hit me. Was Henry playing tricks on this guy too? So, I walked back in and asked if he was losing track of his tools.

"It's unbelievable!" he said. "I put my screwdriver down on the floor behind me and it disappears."

Definitely Henry.

"Just a moment." I said.

I stepped out of the room. Summoning my strongest expletive I said, "*Fuck off, Henry! This guy is trying to do us a favour!*"

Then, after a few moments of reflection, it occurred to me that Henry was a musician and would have wanted the piano tuned. So, I asked him if there was a spirit in the piano. His answer was '*Yes*'. I asked if there were more than one, '*Yes*', again. As it turned out there were several. My assumption is the creative interface between the players and the instrument is an opening to the spirit world.

But back to the story. I thanked Henry for his diligence, apologized for yelling at him and returned to the room. I cautiously explained this scenario to the piano tuner, who to his credit, didn't blanch. I then lit a candle and cleared the piano of spirits.

The piano went back together … like butter.

And then there was the barbecue incident. This was several years after Henry's death but I marked his death and birthdays each year by lighting a candle. This one year, I had decided to barbecue a steak for myself. A rare occasion. However, the propane tank needed to be replaced. I had a reserve tank and proceeded to thread the connector on. In spite of several attempts, it would not thread properly at all.

I was very frustrated. I then recalled that my whole day had been a litany of things that malfunctioned, fell over, dropped to the floor or couldn't be located. The barbecue was the last straw. I wondered what in hell could be so off about this day … when it struck me. "Wait a minute, what day is this?"

It turned out that it was the anniversary of Henry's death. I had completely forgotten it and apologized to him.

The propane tank connected immediately.

A FEW YEARS LATER, WHEN I was living in Newfoundland, I became aware that Henry didn't seem to be around any longer. I contacted the friend he appeared to the night he died. She told me he had 'walked in" to a French-speaking black man's body.

"He'd love that." I said facetiously.

But about two months later Henry came to me one afternoon. I greeted him and asked how he could be there when he was in this other man's body.

"*He's sleeping.*" Henry said.

Think about it.

WALK-INS

FROM MY OWN EXPERIENCE, A walk-in can happen when a person is in a high state of fear. It is then an opening for the entry of another spirit. Either the spirit or the person who experiences a 'walk-in' usually has an attribute that the person in fear needs, such as courage. I have never seen or heard of a 'walk-in' that is negative, but I am open to that revelation, nor do I fully comprehend why the spirit who walks-in is available to do so.

ONE CLIENT SESSION STANDS OUT. A psychologist I worked with contacted me about a client who had recurring World War II dreams and memories of being a terrified pilot who felt completely helpless. The client was himself a retired Airforce enlisted man. The mechanics of how this may happen are difficult to comprehend. The retired client was too young to have been in WWII. Remember that there is no linear time on the other side. So, what I sense happened was the spirit of the young, terrified pilot had exited his body and then 'walked into' the life of the competent retired pilot. Once he knew about what was happening in those dreams, they ceased.

Shortly after that session, I happened to see a documentary about WWII pilots. The British were so desperate for pilots, they were sending young men into the air with minimal training … sometimes it was just a taxi down the runway and how to move the controls for take-off and landing. No airborne experience. Of course, they were terrified.

WHENEVER I PASS A BARBER shop or a hair salon with a sign outside saying "Walk-ins welcome," I chuckle. Do they have any idea whom they might be inviting?

THE ALIENS, ONCE AGAIN

AT AGE FIFTY-ONE, I WAS in Atlanta, Georgia seeing friends. Theirs was a very loving long-term relationship that seemed to affect everyone around them. I left their house feeling high on the bounty of their love. As I started my vehicle up and turned on the radio, I heard Barry White's, "Can't Get Enough Of Your Love Babe."

Damn right. I raised the volume as I was turning out of their driveway and onto Rock Spring Rd. There were two cars approaching at quite a distance from me on my right. To my left there was another car about a block and half ahead of me. Suddenly in the process of turning, I thought I saw my brains, which appeared as a motherboard, flying out from the top of my head and up into the sky. A strange and very familiar feeling started to permeate my being.

Immediately, I knew what was coming and shouted, "Oh no! No. No. No." out loud.

It didn't help. Several minutes later, I have no idea how long in fact, I 'came to'.

There were no cars anywhere in view. The radio was playing different music and my body felt as I had been on a drug trip.

I had experienced another abduction, but this time I was driving.

Yet, I was still in my lane, albeit about 1,500 feet further down the road. I checked my speed, my distance from the curb and the traffic around me constantly. I was definitely altered and feeling quite paranoid. I carefully talked myself back to where I was staying and went straight to bed.

I SAW A VERY GIFTED chiropractor I knew the next morning who confirmed that my energy field was, in fact, upside down.

But why was this happening? Why now? I hadn't had an experience for decades and here I was in my early fifties and worse, I was driving.

I couldn't let this happen again. I drove straight back to Canada the next morning. When I arrived back two friends came over and confirmed that I was still in shock. I was ashen.

I then decided to confer with a guide or two who had often surfaced for me. When I asked for assistance removing the access, I was told very clearly that I was the only one to do that, but they would be right with me. I felt helpless in front of these entities, but I knew deep inside that I was truly the only one who could change this. I was also instinctively aware that this was a life-altering, teaching moment for me.

With great trepidation but nonetheless armed with determination, I set up a safe space for myself and called the aliens in.

To my amazement, they showed up.

They appeared to be grey in colour and quite short.

When I stated to them that I was demanding the abductions stop they told me that I had agreed to be available for them. (!!)

I said that I was now rescinding that agreement. They protested. I insisted again. It went back and forth between us one more time, then, in a flash they were gone.

IN READING DOLORES CANNON'S BOOKS several years later, about the results of her hypnosis sessions with abductee clients, I learned that the aliens were doing surgery and making adjustments to our bodies so that we would survive being on the planet.

Since I rescinded the initial 'agreement', I have had fifteen surgeries. When I realized this, I attempted to reinstate the original agreement but without any success.

For those who are skeptical about abductee experiences, I simply remind them that it didn't happen to them, so how could they possibly have a reference for the experience?

WHO ARE WE, REALLY?

AM I A MULTI-DIMENSIONAL COLLECTION of experiences walking around in a pressurized suit we call a body?

Am I a composite of my past lives, the present and the future?

If time isn't linear, which is what I believe, then my past and future can be accessed in the same moment given the ability to move through the thin veil that separates them.

Just as I decide to try this at will, it happened spontaneously with a client. I find I am soon able to access a so-called "past life" experience with ease but the future I connect with in others is entirely conditional upon the choices they subsequently make for themselves.

Therefore, the future is comprised of unlimited possibilities in a constant state of readiness. Or is it?

My life appeared to be pre-determined when I eliminated the control of my brain. But then what is a brain? My wisdom appeared to come from elsewhere in my body, at times it seemed to be in the air surrounding me.

Is the purpose of the brain to collect experiences in order to protect and inform the whole being?

I found that I was questioning my whole life and the assumptions I had made about it and me. Was I even a solid? I felt that 'a collection of atoms in constant movement' best reflected my understanding. Between the atoms lay the possibility of real change I felt, yet an illness brings a hard-edged version of reality into a demanding focus.

FIRST CLIENT

AFTER TAKING MY FIRST LEVEL in Reiki, I received a call from Anita asking me if I would be interested in volunteering to do Reiki for a woman with leukemia who was in a nearby hospital. I agreed immediately but was also curious about how it would transpire.

The woman had given birth to a daughter just a few months before her diagnosis. She had already lost a leg to the leukemia. However, she responded positively to the work and asked me to return. I felt honoured. Her leukemia was the aggressive version and her prognosis wasn't good.

Over the progress of a few weeks, she had declined to the point where the end of her life was imminent. Then, I received a call from her husband that she was nearing the end. I ran over.

She was unconscious and intubated but still breathing. I sat there and held her arm. A healer I didn't know was on her other arm.

As I closed my eyes, she appeared, lost in thought, on a classic stone garden bench. It was situated on the brow of a hill overlooking a large endless valley in what appeared to be the glow of moonlight. I sat beside her and asked her what was happening for her.

"*I don't know if I should go or stay.*" She said.

I explained that it was still her choice but if she were to stay she would have limited expression given the state of her physical body.

But then there was her daughter and her husband to consider. I also found myself saying that If she decided to go I would accompany her across. I had never done this before, yet I 'knew' I could.

My consciousness drew me back into the room. Her Mother said that she was going to drown in her own fluid. You could hear it. When I returned to the bench on the hill she had stood up (her leg had reappeared) and was walking straight ahead into the moonlit night.

I heard her Mother say, "She's gone."

I had mixed emotions. She had died which was very sad for everyone around her, including me. She was young and had everything to live for, yet I felt quietly elated for her passage.

She was my first 'client' experience. Once again, I was left questioning the nature of life.

WHAT IS DEATH?

ON A SIMPLISTIC LEVEL, IT is the cessation of life. My own experience is that it is also another beginning and not a sad one at that.

WHEN ELEANOR MOORE WAS PASSING away, I had heard that her hospital room was filled with a golden dust in the air. Physicians would visit just in order to stand in the extraordinary energy that surrounded her.

I was advised by Anita not to send healing energy at Eleanor's request. I respected that until the day she passed over when my curiosity got the better of me.

What I 'saw' was a scrambled television screen looking like the early days of television antennas and bad reception. Then I heard her voice.

"I'm okay dear. I don't need assistance."

I stopped immediately.

A few years later the understanding came to me.

A man named Bill Spears, who was working closely with AIDS patients in New York City, had been sitting with a friend who was no longer conscious and about to pass over. The man's partner and sister were also sitting by the bedside.

Bill advised them to say everything they had ever failed to express to him because he could still hear.

His monitor had flat-lined. But when they repeated the words "I love you." the heart monitor detected activity. Each time they uttered those words, his heart reacted. Finally, he passed over completely.

Bill took the patient's partner to the rooftop lounge while the hospital staff attended the body.

He said to Bill, "If only I could get a sign that he was okay."

Immediately, fireworks exploded in the sky above them over the Hudson River.

"Is that enough of a sign for you?" asked Bill.

It was undeniable. Now I knew why Eleanor had requested no assistance. It could hold her back.

LOVE HAS ENORMOUS POWER. IT can extend life when all hope is lost. But the reverse is also true. Relatives who attend the dying and are determined not to let go, can delay the onset of the inevitable in spite of excruciating pain and mental distress. It can be a very selfish act.

I have learned that the spirit of the dead can visit those they love at will. Even in advance of their departure their spirits can visit loved ones. Once across to the other side, they aren't immediately aware of the lack of physical limitations, but it occurs to them after a time. They often use insects and birds to communicate to the living. They signal their presence by turning lights on and off, causing old clocks to chime and filling the air with smells that are identified with them … cigarette or pipe smoke, incense, wood shavings, baking bread or a signature perfume. They can also make familiar sounds happen … a doorbell, strains of music and the sound of their voices calling out. They can comfort with a hug or an arm around the shoulder, a tousling of the hair or a sense of them lying next to you in bed. They can also communicate through memories and thought.

They are actually present and witness the progress of the lives of those they love but without the encumbrance of physical bodies, linear time, mortgage payments, meals to prepare, grass to cut and those innumerable tasks and duties we encounter in day-to-day life. They have been released to fully express their love. It is true freedom.

MY FRIEND, THE LATE MARY WACHTER, whom I will reference again later, worked as a nurse in a Veteran's Affairs Hospital in Phoenix, Arizona. She was often asked to train new nurses on her shift.

In one instance, a nurse trainee came running up to her because the water taps kept turning on and the buzzer was pressed in the room where a patient had died the night before. Yet, the room was vacant. She was terrified.

Mary, simply took her down the hall to the former patient's room, told her to wait in the hall, then entered the room. As she walked in, she noticed that the window was closed. So, she said in a voice loud enough for the trainee to hear,

"I'm sorry. We forgot to leave your window open. Let me do that for you. Now, if there is anything else you need, just press the buzzer."

The taps were no longer turned on. The buzzer ceased ringing.

This is a good example of the confusion spirits experience when they pass over. They often have no idea what they are capable of without the limitations of a body. They can move through walls, space and time. Mary had a rule she shared with a Pima Indian nurse named Percy, that they would always leave a window open when someone passed over. Unfortunately, hospitals no longer have windows that open, so a Shamanic intervention can be timely and appropriate.

CONTACTING SPIRITS

WHAT FOLLOWS IS AN EXCERPT from my website. It is from a client I identify only as Moira G. She posted it initially on Facebook.

> *This Mother's Day, I would like to say a public thank you to Bernard Morin because I believe in the healing power of sharing our stories.*
>
> *I was lucky enough to have a Reiki session with you about 20 years ago, an experience which would plant the seed for what was to become a rather long but interesting journey towards healing. I had been struggling for a long time with my mother's death when I met you and asked you if you could contact her for me. You did, and to this day I continue to treasure that unbelievable experience (unbelievable because I've been a skeptic on and off and it took even me a long time to believe it actually happened despite the tangible sensations I felt that day).*
>
> *That experience would become a pivotal moment for me in changing my understanding of this universe, and it gave me a glimpse into the possibility of finding some light in what had become a very dark existence for me. It was confirmation of my closeted belief that there is more to this world than meets the eye and it brought me comfort at a time when I was quite lost.*

The world had been a scary place for me for many years before that experience (and would continue to be even after) because my spirit had been crushed (not only by my mother's death but also by other events too) and even though I continued to struggle to find my way for years afterwards, I believe that if you hadn't given me that glimmer of hope, that glimpse into the magic that exists within the realms of the unseen, I might never have arrived at this infinitely more peaceful place that I am finally beginning to find myself in.

There is so much emphasis put on our 'mind and body' health yet without a spiritual component, life is filled with so much unnecessary suffering for many. I am grateful to people like you.

MORE RECENTLY, THE FATHER OF a good friend was close to death. He had been in and out of hospital and a retirement residence but he was always brought back from the brink by medical intervention.

Then his second youngest son, whom I will refer to as J, died of an overdose of recreational drugs. The family was in chaos. Should they tell the Father or not? But the hospital discharged him to the family home once more which meant they had no choice but to tell him since the rest of the family had arrived from out of country to support each other over J's tragic death.

I was asked to check in on J on the other side soon after he passed. He was still recovering from the overdose that ended his life. When I checked in with him two days later, he told me he was waiting for his Dad to arrive there … so he knew he would be passing over soon. The family had been deeply religious so there was an unspoken concern that the brother would not end up in the same place as the Father since J was gay.

Then the decision was made to take the Father off all meds other than pain-killers. He passed over in three days. I was asked to check in on him to see how he was. It took the Father a few days to overcome the effect of his painkillers, but eventually he had this big smile on his face … the turmoil and chaos were over.

When I checked on J, he had buried his face in the crook of his Fathers' shoulder and chest. I asked him how he was and he said, "*I finally have my Father all to myself.*" I started to tear up.

When I told this to my friend, his sister, she exhaled. He had been the second youngest. Eleven months after his birth, the youngest was born and J was often left in a playpen by himself. His Father, had been a salesperson who was away a lot. The story now made sense to me and brought comfort to the family. It left me curious whether this ache in his being for his Father was responsible for his addiction to drugs and alcohol. It seems likely.

THE SHAMANIC SELF REVEALED

IN 2010, I EXPERIENCED A bout of pancreatitis which was a first for me. I found myself struggling with severe pain in the very crowded Emergency waiting room of a large major hospital in Toronto.

After four hours I was finally admitted and my complete medical history and symptoms were taken down. I was asked the same questions once again by the intern who attended me once I was assigned a bed. I then saw the rather arrogant doctor who was overseeing the intern. He asked me the identical questions once again. This was now the third time I had repeated my medical history. I have asthma and sleep apnea which I learned are important to be stated clearly. The line of questioning kept pursuing a suspicion that I was a binge drinker. Anyone who knows how little alcohol I consume would find that quite amusing, but I was in a lot of pain and doing my best to reply with patience. I was kept in overnight. The next day the same doctor came into the room and was surrounded by several student interns that the doctor was teaching. My pain had diminished considerably. I heard him state that he would be prescribing Oxycodone. Given the reputation of the drug, I was nervous but followed up as he directed and then went home. I had taken one pill at the hospital and was directed to take another four hours after arriving home. I was exhausted and fell asleep shortly after arriving home. My sleep was quite erratic and unsettled so I decided to sit up, but then dosed off.

To my utter surprise, I was witnessing myself from a distance of about four feet but from a standing point-of-view. Yet, I was asleep.

Into my consciousness I heard the words "*Bernie, you aren't breathing.*" I immediately snapped back into my body and gasped thereby filling my lungs with air.

As I sat there wondering how that could possibly happen, I started to dose off once more. I quickly became conscious that the same cessation of breathing was about to happen again.

Concerned, I got up and logged onto my computer to research Oxycodone. More than a few sites stated that it should never be prescribed for people with asthma and sleep apnea.

I was alarmed and quickly looked up how long the drug stays in the system. I had to stay awake for four hours, in spite of being exhausted by the previous twenty-four hours. But, more significantly I was curious about how I was able to witness myself from outside my body, yet alone issue a warning to my consciousness.

Obviously, I was being monitored by some higher intelligence, and yet it most definitely felt like it was authentically me. The feeling that I was taken care of swept through my being. It wasn't up to my brain alone to be responsible for my physical state. A far greater intelligence seemed to be attending my well-being.

WHEN I JOURNEY SHAMANICALLY, I am able to travel anywhere to any time in the past or in the future. I am able to witness the dreams people have as they describe them. Yet in all that time, I had never seen myself as a separate physical entity.

A very gifted student of mine had once described how, after one of my classes on Shamanism, she noticed that she was sitting in the back seat of her car watching herself as she was driving home from the class. I now knew, first-hand what she had experienced.

The more I became familiar with Shamanism, the more I realized that Reiki had a lot in common with it. The third symbol which is used in distant healing creates a shamanic opening. You can work directly with people at a distance as if they were right in front of you. Your hands start to buzz with the energy as soon as you locate the person you are contacting.

MY PARTNER, HENRY, AND I spent one Christmas in New Mexico. When I picked him up at the airport, he told me that his school's Principal was in the hospital with cancer. He then asked me if I would send healing to him. A little later in our hotel room, I prepared myself to send healing. But in order to do that you need a person's name and where they are. We knew his name, but my partner didn't know where he lived nor which hospital he was in. So, I framed his location as Principal of a certain high school but currently in hospital. I waited a couple of minutes then my hands started buzzing. I decided to see more clearly where he was. I immediately found myself in his hospital room. I looked around and recognized the shape and colour of the room. It was in Credit Valley Hospital. I had worked on someone there before. I could have walked out the door and checked the room number. I looked at Ed lying in the bed. He was intubated, hooked up to several machines and clearly was only allowed restricted visitors. I gave him a Reiki treatment. I mused about the possibility of not being able to return to the motel room in Arizona, yet I knew I could. I reported back to Henry who confirmed with me later after we arrived home, that Ed was indeed in that specific hospital.

It was all the confirmation I needed.

THE DANGER OF EGO

WHEN ONE IS RAISED FEELING "less than" in life, the arrival of new-found abilities can easily lead to an exaggerated sense of self-importance. The ego (uncapitalized) is the expression of the self. However, the Ego (capitalized), defines the exaggerated self.

This was me. I had spent my life vying for self-importance. I craved the acknowledgment I was missing.

In my experience, nothing shuts down the flow of energy faster than Ego, particularly with energy work such as Reiki. What we are engaged to do as practitioners is to open ourselves up to the natural intelligence of the energy and get out of the way. The energy is summoned by the patient/client. The Ego siphons off an amount of the energy in order to serve the needs of the practitioner. It is exhausting after a period of time. Failure to recognize this can elicit a tough lesson. Yet my previous work in advertising, rewarded the strong expression of Ego with advancement, money and praise.

I was confused.

Is there a natural role for the Ego in healing?

I had to get out of my own way. It's a very humbling lesson when you feel you've just found (or re-found) your purpose in life.

WHERE DO WE COME FROM?

THIS IS A LOADED TOPIC, but my personal experience was very clear. I decided to journey to where I came from, my origins if you will. I knew where I would go after I die, but where was I from?

With this as my focus, I journeyed outward into space, into the Universe. Though I wasn't the one navigating, there was a definite trajectory occurring. I noticed a stream of spirits on my right going through an obscure entity that for lack of any other description, must be God for them.

After they streamed through this entity they continued to Earth with physical bodies, though they were indistinct as yet.

But clearly, I was not from that stream, which explained why I felt no relationship to the concept of 'God'. This was a complete surprise. However, in my quiet moments of reflection I was aware of a guide I call Sananda, the Sanscrit name for "Jesus" or Yahweh. That felt like a fit for me but the name "Jesus" was too wrought with issues to even say. I am having difficulty writing it even now. I find I can communicate with Sananda directly and without any of the associated Christian dogma or blasphemy. It is a clean communication. I am never preached to, criticized, made to feel guilt or remorse nor made to feel 'less than' in any way.

Sananda exists to aid in my work whenever I express the need. No conditions ever, no questions asked. The realm of angels and archangels that many people refer to also has no reference in my experience, yet I willingly listen to the folks who offer advice from their angelic sources. It's personal and specific to the individual.

When I am confronted by a Christian Evangelist saying, "*Have you accepted Christ as your personal savior?*"

My answer is, "*He told me that it's my job to save myself.*"

And it is. I just substitute that loaded name with Sananda.

When you hear it spoken, Sananda sounds like the love it is.

Back to the journey. I entered what can only be described as an amorphous space of swirling, opaque and coloured light.

Then, a voice inside my head welcomed me home.

I asked where this was and the answer I heard was, "*This is where you were brought into form.*"

My name for this 'place' is "The Conscious Unmanifest."

AS BIZARRE AS THIS SEEMS, it matches imagery from other journeys I had with Eleanor and Anita. I once ended up around a large oval viewing portal. There were several of us looking down upon a planet through this portal. What was clear to me, as we mustered a creation in our minds, it thus manifested in front of us in the portal. I questioned whether this was just my Ego playing tricks on me but was assured that this was real. However, the time frame relative to our linear time wasn't made known to me. This underscores the responsibility I have for my thoughts. They may precede manifestation … and my life had been showing me just that. I had to control and to clear any fear I had, any misgivings about myself or negative thought patterns for the sake of the work in which I am called to participate.

ENERGY

IN MY EXPERIENCE, OUR WORLD is full of energy, a life force that surrounds and suffuses us.

Take a moment to connect with it. Stand or sit in the middle of the room, close your eyes and pause for a minute. Then raise your dominant hand, fingers spread, then position it so it faces a wall. With your eyes still closed, slowly move your hand around the room. The most sensitive area of your hand will be the skin between your fingers.

Did you notice a difference when you moved your hand past a door, a window, a plant or a piece of art?

WHEN I FIRST CONNECTED WITH Reiki in my personal practice, I would lie on the floor with my hands on my chest. After a few minutes, my whole body would be buzzing. It felt as if I were flying. The only parallel experience I can liken it to would be a drug trip. I rarely experimented with drugs, yet on subsequent occasions when the opportunity to do marijuana arose, I found it got in the way. My life, as I was now experiencing it was 'trip' enough.

Similar to this sensory awareness, when working on someone,

my hands — particularly my dominant hand — would start to buzz and was magnetized to particular places on their bodies. Those places would correspond directly to the observations I had noticed many years ago in England (*see* pages 14–16). Not only that, I found I could sense deeply into those areas and was able to identify the issues that were lodged there. After bringing what I was sensing to the attention of my client, the issues would spontaneously leave the body, often accompanied by an emotional release.

Issues that had plagued people for years were melting away in the space of an hour. In fact, as the years progressed, the time decreased. I am in awe of the process.

Before commencing a session, I would always ask of Spirit that the person receive what they need in the time allotted with no residue of incomplete processes.

But who was Spirit? Was 'Spirit' connected to my gut feeling? And what effect did Spirit have on my work?

Good questions … with no conclusive answers, at least not yet.

TREE SPIRITS

TREES HAVE A RECOGNIZABLE ENERGY and a spirit life.

I first came to this awareness when I lived in a house surrounded by woods. I noticed that one older tree, a cedar, was within striking distance of the house should there be a strong storm. I had it taken down as a precaution and decided to speak to the tree about my reasons for doing so.

What really surprised me was that after it was taken down, I could still 'see' the energy in the form of the tree for a few weeks after it was removed. Not only that but birds would fly around it and falling snow would also move around that energy form and not through it. The energy itself looked like heat waves rising from the surface of a hot highway. It was particularly noticeable flowing off and around trees that were in bloom.

It was the same phenomenon I had noticed coming off fresh fruit and flowers in my youth.

My world was transforming. My childhood was starting to make sense.

A FEW YEARS LATER I was walking with a friend through the Joyce Kilmer Memorial Forest, a magnificent old-growth forest in North Carolina. As we walked, I distinctly heard voices speaking in hushed tones, almost whispers … yet my friend heard nothing. We appeared to be alone. There were no other cars in the parking area nor had we run into anyone else on the trails.

The trees, I then realized, had to be talking to each other. I stopped and addressed one very old tree next to the path and asked 'it' to speak with me.

To my amazement, a low male voice spoke back to me though my friend couldn't hear it.

To me at least, it was the spirit of the tree.

The whole forest was alive with tree spirits in conversation with each other … not only that but they appeared to be speaking English. Was that how my brain interpreted it or am I able to understand 'Tree'?

Is every living thing enspirited, I wondered?

I was once more full of questions.

I SHARED THIS STORY WHEN I was teaching in Atlanta, then a man in the class shared his own incredible experience.

He had been camping with his wife. After a long drive they arrived at their next site. He decided to rest awhile under the shade of an oak tree. As he sat there, he told his wife that the tree was talking to him. He thanked the tree for providing shade and support for his respite. It then occurred to him to ask the tree if there was anything he could do for it.

The answer was "*Yes. What is it like to run?*"

Think about that for a moment.

The tree … again apparently communicating in English, was curious about another species' experience.

The man then gathered what he felt was the spirit of the tree on his back and ran about fifty yards, straight ahead. When he returned the tree spirit to where he had been sitting, the tree said. "*Thank you. I always wondered what that felt like.*"

My next thoughts were whether every tree was enspirited or was it just the older ones? Again, the wildfire of questions consumed my consciousness.

AS I PROGRESSED IN MY personal Shamanic practice, I came to understand that all plants, bushes and shrubs included, have a spirit. I was able to dialogue with a tree about whether it was safe to leave it standing and got definitive answers. In one class a participant journeyed to the cherry tree in the yard of her childhood home. I had directed the class to ask about memories the tree may hold. In this case the tree reminded her of how she and her brothers would play in it and how one time, the tree prevented her fall. The participant had entirely forgotten about it … but the tree remembered.

So, they not only have spirit, they have memory. Are they male or female, do they have progeny they recognize, what other plants do they communicate with?

So many questions.

SPIRIT

WHAT OR WHO IS SPIRIT? This question plagued me for years. It was right there when I asked for assistance, right there when I had a question while working on a client, and right there whenever I went into that internal stillness where all the answers are found. It was simply a matter of knowing what to ask. Was spirit inside of me or outside? Is Spirit actually me, or perhaps my higher self? Further, am I separate from my higher self?

This instigates another line of questioning. Is Spirit in everything and everywhere I look? If Spirit is me, am I in everything I see and experience? Am I everyone and everywhere all at once?

Is my sense of Spirit the same as someone else's? When I die will Spirit greet me? Again, is Spirit actually, intrinsically me?

How can I figure this out? Do I even need to know the answers to these questions? Can these questions simply be the 'mystery' of life, the unknowable with which I need to find comfort, much like change?

THE REAL DEAL

IN 1985, WHILE STILL IN advertising, a few years prior to my formal involvement in Reiki and Shamanism, I purchased a large Arts and Crafts mansion on an island in Stony Lake in Eastern Ontario. It was built in the early 1900's but was in a state of great decay.

I am not sure that I had a choice in the purchase.

I had been looking for an escape from the AIDS trauma that was so prevalent in the city. I had invited a friend, the aforementioned Scott Cline, to share my apartment. His partner had already succumbed to the disease and Scott was left spinning his wheels. I also had a long-time friend with AIDS living with his partner two floors above me. They, too, were spinning with fear because one of them was now exhibiting symptoms. I would deliver food to them up the backstairs. But everywhere I turned, every phone call, every friend I bumped into was brimming with fear. I needed an escape to a sense of calm, thus the island.

I saw the island initially from a boat and my reaction to it was profound. It felt like an earthquake … yet I was on a boat.

So, yes, with that kind of a signal, I ended up buying it.

It needed … everything and, in the end, all the money I had.

But the memories it fostered still endure. I gathered an intentional community around me to live there in the summers and to help fix it up. It was a mammoth undertaking. But we weren't alone.

Around the end of the third year a conversation erupted among the island community in which we spoke about the unusual 'things' that had been happening.

We had never spoken about it as a group before. Eventually, as experiences spilled out, we had to admit that we had uninvited company there. We had ghosts.

IT'S A LONG STORY, BUT the shortened version of it is that martini glasses shot out of the cupboard as if from a slingshot whenever someone would mention the name of the woman for whom the house was built. When I purchased it, we had ten of those Martini fifties-style glasses. Eventually we were down to one.

Footsteps trod the halls at night, the old grand piano in the living-room was known to play in the middle of the night, curtains often stood out at forty-five-degree angles even when the windows were closed. In one specific bedroom, a dream about a baby drowning off the boathouse kept recurring to the house member who slept there, but she didn't have that same dream, when she was at home. In fact, no-one ever slept well in that room.

I too had barely slept since I purchased the property. My recurring dreams were about worthlessness, failure and madness. A distinctive female voice would yell my failures at me in my slumber state. We were often followed upstairs by a rustling sound on the stair railings. An image of a man falling off the stair railing onto the foyer floor below appeared to one person. An image of an angry female revealed herself in a mirror much to the horror of a guest. At the boathouse one evening, the most skeptical pair among us felt an eerie cold presence sweep in like a cold, damp breeze yet it was a hot, sticky night. They were spooked by it and ran up to the main house.

They were skeptics no longer.

Yet, the last straw was drawn when a guest awoke to a presence of an angry female in early 1900's dress standing at the doorway to her bedroom, hands on hips barring any exit. The guest awoke later that night to the same presence on top of her, trying to strangle her in the bed.

It was time.

A CHANNELER AND A WITNESS/OVERSEER were hired. A young child was channeled almost immediately in a closet used to store linens. She kept repeating, "*I want my dolly. I want my Mommy.*" The channeler and overseer were able to get her to depart quite easily.

The second spirit they encountered was the woman for whom the house was designed and built. She was most definitely the offending female spirit. She kept repeating that I must leave, that, "*It's my house not his house!*" She admitted to invading my dreams, and she also had a knowledge of my scheduled visits to my therapist. So, her awareness obviously wasn't limited to the house.

But something else was holding her there because she adamantly refused to leave. Additionally, a rather formal gentleman in a top hat and morning suit appeared in the dining-room, and was seen on two separate occasions by two different people. He was peering out of the dining-room window as they were climbing the steps to the veranda.

Who was he? How did he fit into the history of the house?

More questions and as yet no answers … except this one. I had been scraping old wallpaper off the attached small cottage called the Commodore's Cottage and found a drawing on the original plaster. It was drawn with the broad lead of a carpenter's pencil. It depicted a woman who looked like a governess in early 1900's dress and hat. She held the hand of a young girl with a doll in her other hand. A dialogue bubble attached to the young girl stated "*I want my mummy.*"

My life was again becoming one very long series of questions.

ENTER THE SHAMAN

A SHAMAN/MEDICINE MAN FROM A nearby First Nation's reserve was then asked to help us out. I won't reveal his name because I have subsequently lost touch with him and have been unable to ask for permission.

Over the first few years, I had heard many stories about the residence and the former occupants from long-time lake residents. I assumed many of them were simply rumours that were passed along between generations. Many of them made no rational sense to me.

On the day that I picked the Shaman up at the landing, the sky was completely clear with no wind whatsoever. After he got in, I turned the boat around and immediately noticed that the sky was now filled with dark, heavy clouds.

"*He's the real deal,*" I thought. "*He can change the weather.*"

WE SAT ON THE VERANDA for a chat. I felt it necessary to explain why I needed to speak with him. I also wanted some form of guarantee that this issue would be gone forever.

His response was profound.

"The guarantee is as strong as your honour (thunder clap) and my honour (another thunder clap)."

Every time he paused there was a clap of thunder. Then the rain came. It whipped in almost on a horizontal angle, yet he didn't flinch and sat there calmly smoking his pipe.

He had already cleared the property a few days beforehand, so this was my opportunity to ask questions. He told me about the main protagonist, who was, in fact, the woman for whom the house had been designed and subsequently built. He chuckled and said that she was quite a handful. She had learned that sex and manipulation were the currency of her power. But her husband had passed over shortly after their dream house was built. She still mourned his loss and was searching for him in the place they both loved. I was in "his" room it turned out. However, one evening years later, she had a dalliance with a visitor. Her Father disapproved of the union, fought with the man and ended up being responsible for pushing him over the stair railing to his death. Thus, the image of the man falling.

I asked him what had happened near the boathouse. He told me a baby had drowned there which, of course, linked up with the dreams one resident had in that problem bedroom. It also turns out, that room had been her bedroom when she was alive.

The Shaman then proceeded to weave together every story I had heard about this magnificent residence. It was truly a tortured history. In asking the questions of him, I would simply ask what happened in a specific location. He would then fill in details with the exact story I had heard, but without any prompting.

Finally, I asked him who was in the dining-room. He answered that it was one of Canada's Prime Ministers.

"Laurier?" came out of my mouth yet I was consciously unaware of the specifics of our history at that time.

The Shaman nodded.

"But why here?" I asked

He replied, "Do you believe in the phrase, we make our own heaven, we make our own hell?"

I replied that I did.

He then said "This is his idea of heaven."

"He is welcome to stay." I replied after a moment of consideration.

"That's what he said about you." He answered.

I was strangely comforted. Subsequent research revealed that the Prime Minister at the time, Sir Wilfrid Laurier, had indeed been a close family friend and visitor on several occasions. The household was also staunchly Methodist, teetotalers and anti-Catholic yet curiously Wilfrid Laurier was a Catholic. Influence and social standing obviously trumped religion. Now I knew why the martini glasses were being broken.

The Shaman also told me that the house and grounds were located on a sacred healing ground for the First Nations people. That information now explained why time had a way of expanding when you were there. A few days felt like a week away, a few hours felt like two days. Visitors lost all track of time and sense of direction when they were there. I have come to recognize that these are the hallmarks of healing energy and sacred places specifically.

AFTER THE SHAMAN'S WORK, THE house felt very different. It was calm and welcoming, even the architecture appeared to take on more pleasing lines.

When I took the Shaman back to the marina and again turned the boat around, the sky had cleared and was cloudless once more.

There is much more to this story, but my personal takeaway was that emotional residue is the reason for the sightings of apparitions. In her case, it was anger, outrage and extreme loss. She knew when I was there and when I wasn't and appeared to be living in the past yet fully aware of the present.

But could she also see the future?

I also wondered what it must be like to be her, something that always piques my curiosity. What nature of chaos inhabited her world after her physical death?

The Shaman's work shifted her offending spirit out of the house. She didn't return. In the case of the Prime Minister, what held him there was his bliss, his heaven. His presence contributed to the sense of calm we would experience there.

The Shaman's ease of facility moving through the layers of history, his ability to see the details clearly and the way he was able to move the weather was more than impressive.

I felt I had just been handed a crucial course in life.

Personal trauma aside, my journey had just been kick-started.

NEEN

A FEW YEARS LATER AT Stony Lake, I had the privilege of assisting a woman who was dying of lung cancer. Neen had an extraordinary bearing and a very warm heart. I was unable to shift the cancer as it had progressed too far, but I could offer comfort and a degree of physical ease from her symptoms. She was also very aware of when I worked on her in distance which was encouraging.

Her personal preference was to die at their cottage on Stony Lake. It entailed oxygen tanks, a hospital bed and pain medication. However, the weather was making this part of her journey very difficult. It was sticky hot, very close with humidity and no form of breeze for relief.

After one visit, her daughter, Mary, accompanied me down to the dock where my boat was moored. She expressed to me her frustration with the weather just before I was about to leave.

I asked her what ideal weather would be like.

"Well it would be nice if it were cooler." She said.

"Exactly what temperature?" I asked.

"Seventy-two degrees.'

"A clear or overcast sky?" I added.

"Slightly overcast."

"Wind or no wind?"

"A light breeze." she said.

"For how long?"

"As long as Mum is alive."

"Okay. Now we will put this request out to the Weather Spirits but do it with absolute resolve. Do not entertain the possibility of a 'no' or even a 'maybe' as a response."

We stood at the end of the dock and quietly expressed our intentions.

The next day, as requested, it was seventy-two degrees, lightly overcast with a hint of a breeze. Just what Neen needed.

I was visiting that day when her doctor arrived. I asked him what the weather was like in Peterborough and he said, "Unbearably hot and sticky, but it's nice here!"

I asked him where the weather changed.

"Right at the landing."

Mary and I exchanged glances. He had arrived on the south shore of the lake.

The day after that someone arrived who had just been shopping in Apsley north of the lake. She complained how unbearably hot and humid it was. I asked her where it changed.

"Right at the marina here at the lake." She replied.

She had arrived on the northern shore of the lake.

More knowing glances exchanged with Mary.

The weather was distinctly different right over the lake but nowhere else.

Neen passed away at the cottage as she wished. The day after, it was hot and sticky again. We thanked the Weather Spirits.

I would never ask the Weather Spirits to intervene except when the circumstances are extreme or life-threatening.

BECOMING AN EMPATH

I USED TO GO ON family fishing trips. I wasn't drawn to the fishing at all, I was drawn to the comradery of family.

Parts of the fishing culture were a significant problem for me. I found that I empathized with the frogs that were to be used as bait and were often transported in plastic bags. I felt for the fish who would be yanked violently out of their world by a hook in their mouths and into a foreign atmosphere without life-giving water passing over their gills. Then they would be tossed back often after a time or be dragged on a stringer off the side of the boat.

I assumed that the reason behind my sensitivity was because I just wasn't male enough. But after I was introduced to Shamanism, I gained an entirely different perspective on it.

I am an empath.

FISH, FROGS, TREES AND HUMANS were all within my purview of empathic understanding unless hunting and fishing were for sustenance. In that case, it became even more important to relate to the spirit of the animal that your existence depended upon.

A DIRECTION EMERGES

I WAS BEGINNING TO ACCEPT that what I intended or asked for, if it were for the highest good … happened. On any occasion when my requests were thwarted or simply didn't happen, I came to realize that I had my own personal growth to go through first. I was lacking an awareness or an understanding of my place in the world in which I found myself.

This process wasn't without its frustrations. On many an occasion, I wished there had been a manual or a memo telling me what to do or where to direct my attention. I had to learn patience and to accept that I was always in the right place at the right time … not an easy demeanor to accept for someone who felt that life was either on hold or required suppression for several decades.

My experience of Shamanic visions with Ruth, my experience of finding a sense of home and emotional release with Anita, my extraordinary experiences and confirmation with Eleanor, my success with intentions in France, my observations of people in England (*see* pages 14–16) with Diana Chappell, my experience of listening to the power of thoughts and words by Diane Brown, my awareness of my empathic ability with trees, people, weather and animals … all fit the mysterious puzzle of my emerging life. I simply had to trust my instincts and to allow the natural pace of my life to unfold.

THE WORK

MY WORK WITH OTHERS STARTED with working on myself. In fact, it never stops. I am my own instruction book.

As I am introduced to a new client, I first tune into to how I am feeling. I check to make sure that I am grounded and feel clear mentally.

When presented with a client either face-to-face, on the telephone, Facetime or Zoom, I go through the same checklist on myself prior to the session. In that way, if anything changes within me, during the session, I immediately know that my client's body or spirit is communicating directly with mine, a phenomenon known as "hook-up" or "tracking." Then, chances are I will know what the issue is they are dealing with whether they tell me or not.

This is why it's imperative to work on yourself.

AS I STARTED TO ACT upon requests to teach Shamanism, I will admit to my shock at the response from the people I taught. They all seemed to have specific animal incidences occur around them prior to the class. I began to accept that the energy for this work was ripe. People were ready for it. I too, had animal experiences as I approached this work. Many times, a wolf or a coyote would run across my path or the road ahead of me, even in heavy traffic. A hawk would often appear above me or cross my vision when driving.

ADDITIONALLY, SHAMANISM WAS A LARGE part of the healing sessions I conducted on behalf of others. Eventually, I used Shamanism exclusively as a way of seeing and interpreting the issues people were facing when they came to me. More precisely, my experience of Shamanism was suffused with Reiki. Clients were left with the same sense of peace and ease they experienced with my Reiki treatments. There was a marked difference for me though. My sessions now appeared to peak and to conclude at the twenty-minute mark. If we went into another round of healing, it too, ended after twenty minutes. I then experimented with terminating the session at twenty minutes but continuing at a later date. In that way, the content of the twenty-minute healing session could be inculcated into the memory of both the brain and the body. I would leave the date of the follow-up session up to the discretion of the client with an eye to fostering their self-awareness.

Sessions would start initially with a conversation. At one point in that conversation, I would get a 'hit', an energetic burst or signal, that would tell me to pursue what had just been said. I would ask my Spirit Animal to show me the age of first cause of the issue we sought. A number or an image would come into my consciousness which would then lead me to ask the client what happened then. As the recollection unfolded, I started to see a more complete picture. Words and pictures would appear to me that I would convey to the client. The reaction from my client always confirmed that what I saw was accurate and very relevant to the incident being worked on.

Then, almost unconsciously, I envision an energetic field, like a large bubble in front of my client that is free of all of their encumbrances and fears. I then silently encourage them to move forward into that space to experience the lightness that can be theirs.

WORKING WITH ELEANOR MOORE, I learned that the energy generated for healing can be summoned, directed and softened by the practitioner as required by the patient, either unconsciously or not. It will rise to meet the needs of the treatment. It appears to have its own wisdom or is directed by an invisible force precisely as required.

When I started giving Reiki treatments there was a prescribed timing and method of treatment promoted by teachers within the Reiki Alliance. We were taught to place our hands in specific positions for a predetermined period of time on the front of the body, then after asking the client to turn over there were prescribed positions for the back. However, the more I worked with clients the more I realized that turning them over when they were in the middle of emotional release or while they were experiencing extraordinary visions, was far too disruptive to their process.

I had also realized that if I held my hands about 6–8 inches above the body there was an energy field to be found there. If I moved my hands back and forth in that field my hands felt 'magnetized' to specific areas. When I cross-referenced those areas with the awareness I had gained in England (*see* pages 14–16), a story emerged. I would later tell the clients what I had perceived and what issues were related to that area of the body from my own experience. What I had sensed was always relevant and important to the process the client was working through.

Slowly, I began to fully trust where to place my hands. Often when I felt that I 'should' move my hands to another position, they wouldn't move. It was as if they were glued. Eventually I would sense that it was now time to move my hands.

This unconscious signaling always intrigued me.

Reiki is known to increase the sense of heat in the palm of the hands. It is real and at times intense. Clients notice that my hands feel as if they are on fire. Yet the top of my hands feel a normal temperature. My own sense of it is that the energy is channeled through the palms to wherever it is needed. The greater the need, the hotter it is perceived. For me, my hands were hot and buzzing whenever deep healing took place.

Eleanor once said that the heat generated in healing could melt synthetic fibers like nylon. I believed her. A friend who was a caterer used to make chocolate truffles at Christmas. After taking Reiki her hands melted the chocolate in her hands before she could form them properly. She subsequently had to place her hands in ice water in order to work with chocolate.

Unfortunately, I cannot work on myself. It just doesn't work other than the calming effect it provides. This frustration has been a real conundrum in my life and it leaves me wandering in that no-man's land between the medical community and alternative practitioners. For instance, with allergies, I have found far more effective diagnostics and healing in the alternative community. Yet, I can't tell medical professionals how I have achieved my success there. Specifically, I realized that I was experiencing asthma attacks when living in Newfoundland, surrounded by the sea. Significantly, the attacks happened when the wind was coming off the ocean. The medical solution was to give me Ventolin inhalers which are in a saline solution. My condition would worsen until a second Ventolin inhaler was administered and overcame the effect of the salt.

The source was confirmed when I returned to Ontario and ended up following a salt spray truck in advance of a winter storm resulting in another attack. Every medical expert I met had the same answer when I mentioned my suspicion: "*Well, I've never heard of that.*"

Until I met an intern at a major hospital in Toronto after that last particularly difficult attack. He had the wisdom to ask me what I thought it was.

"You may think I'm crazy, but I believe it's airborne saline." I said.

"I don't think you're crazy," he replied. "I have it."

I almost hugged him. He was the first medical practitioner I had met who had the wisdom to ask what I felt it was.

NORMALCY

I WANT TO TAKE A moment here to state that I don't feel special or exceptionally gifted. Nor do I feel I am elevated beyond anyone else who opens themselves up to their full expression and responsibility. My gifts are normal for me. They are just not recognized by a prevailing authority with a certificate or a title. My wish would be to work alongside recognized professionals and be held in equal regard.

Any professional therapist, psychologist, doctor or nurse I have worked with or taught has brought a viewpoint, knowledge and descriptive abilities to the table that has enhanced the work we did together. They have all acknowledged that this work quickens the healing process. The problem they face is finding a way to describe the process to others and to professional associations.

Additionally, everything that happens to you or that you encounter in your life can be a teaching and is often an issue that when acknowledged and accepted, catapults you into awareness and empowerment.

The deeper you mine your own experiences, the more compassionate and understanding you can be for others.

SOUL FRAGMENTS

SOUL FRAGMENTATION HAPPENS FREQUENTLY ... USUALLY because of accidents, surgeries, trauma, intense fear or grief.

Example

I once worked on a health care professional who was involved in a head-on collision. His legs were being crushed by the engine of his car which was now mostly in the passenger compartment. He was losing blood badly but had sufficient consciousness to utter "Break in! Break in!" to the paramedics who first attended him on scene. What that means professionally is to hook up an IV blood source ASAP to counter the loss of blood.

When I worked with him, his body summoned great amounts of energy through me that surged out of my hands. I then became suspicious that he had lost a soul fragment and wasn't feeling like himself aside from his injuries. His eyes had a slightly vacant appearance which is common with soul fragmentation.

I made sure he felt grounded then I asked him to revisit the impending scene of the accident, just before he knew that the collision was imminent. I then asked him to freeze the image and imagine that the cars (his and the crash vehicle that hit him) were made of a rubber that bounced back when struck. I next instructed him to unfreeze the image. After the now innocuous incident transpired, I instructed him to say out loud, "*Oh good, no damage here, no injuries and everything is perfect.*"

It seems hokey I know, but in this way you create a new belief in the cellular memory of the body that counters the original incident. Stress within the body is thereby greatly reduced though not yet fully eliminated.

I then asked him to look around the scene of the accident site for a version of himself that was standing at the side of the road. We were both able to locate that image. The key to identifying soul fragments is that their feet don't touch the ground. They float slightly above it, leaving a shadow under their feet. Next, we worked at moving that fragment of his soul back into his body.

The technique involves having the client hold out her/his/their hands about to hug the fragmented self. Next ask the client to take a long slow breath in as the hands are slowly moved towards the heart centre (sternum). At that point when your client can't take in any more air, the hands should be right at the sternum. The client then forcefully exhales while keeping the hands on the sternum. The soul fragment is typically inculcated into the body. It will be energetically obvious to the client, right down to the feet.

Physical healing can then start at a more rapid pace.

It should be noted that this technique is occasionally difficult with people who are brain-bound, linear left-brain types who are unable to relinquish the control they have given over to their brains. Even then, I have met success.

CLEARING SPIRITS

THE AWARENESS I GAINED FROM my experience with the Shaman when clearing my island residence, was put to good use as I was now being asked to clear land and houses.

Example

When I contact a 'ghost', I start a conversation with them to discover what their history is and why they are stuck. I am always curious. What I understand and believe is that they are simply people without bodies, stuck in emotional turmoil. For me they are soul fragments. They have no idea they are dead. I remind them of it by referring to repetition in daily life.

> Me: "When was the last time you had dinner?"
> Ghost: "Um, hmm I'm not sure."
> Me: "When was the last time you slept?"
> Them: (silence)
> Me: When did you last have a shower or a bath?"
> Them: (silence and confusion)
> Me: "When did you last go to the bathroom?"
> Them: (either no answer or indignance)
> Me: "See, the problem is you're dead, but you're in the wrong

place. Allow me to show you where you should be right now. People are waiting for you."

If there is any reluctance, I make a deal and offer to bring them right back if they aren't comfortable there. I then take them up to a place above the clouds where they are met by relatives and loved ones. It can be very emotional even though initially it sounds a bit disrespectful.

WHENEVER I AM IN EUROPE, I visit Canadian Military Cemeteries. They are often full of soul fragments. One cemetery I encountered in Belgium near Adagen, was atypically unkempt. I wondered if it had been recognized as an official site. I was travelling with a former student.

I felt drawn to the site so nothing else would do but to stop and check it out. As soon as we entered the gates, you could feel the soul fragments everywhere. This is typical when death came without warning. One was under a helmet on the ground and terrified. I could only see his eyes at ground level. Another was walking casually through smoke with his helmet in hand. I asked him what he was doing there. He told me he was looking for his regiment. It took a bit of convincing, but he finally agreed to let me take him up above the clouds to his regiment. In all we took several soul fragments up. Then, as we exited the cemetery, we saw a sign for a Canadian Military Museum. Oddly, it wasn't anywhere on the map, but our curiosity was aroused.

The Museum was a private memorial to the Canadians who liberated that part of Belgium in the Second World War. Surrounding it were remnants of trenches in the field, old Howitzer guns, and a tank. The building was a modern community hall with a bar and an attached diorama. The diorama was incredibly detailed and displayed many WWII artifacts both Canadian and German.

The story of this unofficial museum was that the father of the man who built it told him on his deathbed that they owed the Canadians a big thank you. He had hidden escaping Jews in the basement of his house over the war and was a day away from being discovered when the Canadian liberators came through. He asked his son to build a memorial as a thank you. Knowing how many we lost in the liberation of Europe and having just escorted a few of them up to the light, we were very moved.

The car was silent for the next hour as we drove on.

IN ATLANTA, GEORGIA, I WAS asked to check out an internet café run by an acquaintance. It was in the basement of what was called the old Ford building, a former automotive industrial building. He and several of his friends had said the stairwell felt 'weird'. A friend of mine, upon hearing this, stated that the parking lot for the grocery store next to that building always felt very creepy. The store needed armed guards at the entrance, unusual for the times.

What I noticed when I stepped onto the tarmac of the parking area was a distinct feeling of a lynching. I then 'saw' black people corralled like animals near where the lynching was taking place which was now the parking lot. Small wonder it felt creepy.

When I entered the stairwell of the Ford Building, I could feel the presence. The soul fragment of a tall black man was crouched under the stairs. He appeared to be quite aggressive. I spoke with him about leaving but was met with strong resistance.

I then offered to take him up to the light to show him where it was, then, I would bring him right back. I felt I owed him the option of seeing where he could safely be. He reluctantly agreed.

As I led him up, I looked back and saw that he was bringing three small children behind him, all holding hands. He had obviously been protecting them. When we got to the light, they were all met by grandparents and a woman I assume was the children's mother. It was deeply emotional for me. The feelings stayed with me for weeks.

Subsequent research I heard confirmed that this had been a slave auction area. It's devastating. For how many other places in the American southeast could this be true?

Another example, a friend had asked me to see a house he was considering buying outside of Charles Town, West Virginia. It was a spectacular location overlooking the Shenandoah River.

However, something was impeding his potential purchase. The owner was reluctant, papers were not in order and nothing seemed to flow which might otherwise confirm that he was the right person for this house.

As I walked around the site I was drawn to the basement of the large decrepit federal-style house. When I went inside, it became clear.

In the basement there was a large fireplace where the kitchen had originally been located. Nearby was the soul fragment of a black woman. She told me she had been the slave cook for the original owners and she had been treated badly. I offered to take her "up" to where people were waiting for her. She was adamant in her refusal. When I explored her reluctance further, she revealed that she was protecting the soul fragments of young children. This was again, another very emotional realization for me. She had been so courageous in the face of beatings but had stayed with the children who had themselves been badly beaten. Eventually they all agreed to go "up" where they were met with an enormous outpouring of love. Again, my heart was deeply touched by this for weeks.

My friend subsequently lost all interest in the house. We speculate now whether the need for the clearing was the reason he was attracted to it.

I have had several amazing and disturbing experiences clearing spirits from land and residences. But allow me to pose a few questions and to proffer possible answers from my point of view.

Soul fragments only exist after death if the initial trauma is not or cannot be dealt with. All of the 'ghosts' I have worked with were held in place, by unreconcilable trauma. Sometimes that happens because of extreme trauma prior death and at other times it happens because of impossible and/or highly emotional situations in their lifetime. Those situations create a silo of emotion, a 'ghost' if you will, that is held in that place in perpetuity. That is what I refer to as soul fragments. They affect the places they inhabit in a negative manner from our point of view. The exception is the presence of spirits for whom that particular place was 'heaven'.

Example

A house in the country in the state of Georgia had a problem with fires. When I heard about the fires and then saw the house itself, I knew what had happened. The house was built upon a sacred burial site of the Native tribe who had lived on that land. The site was elevated and near water, two clues to a burial site. I am always cautious and deeply respectful when dealing with native sites. I am in their territory and ritual lands. I always ask for permission to work with them and won't proceed until I hear affirmation.

The spirits resident in this site, one of whom was a chief, were extremely angry. Thus, the history of fires.

When I encounter a native site, such as a burial place, there is more to do. Their 'heaven' is the land they are buried on. If someone has defiled the location intentionally or not, the spirits buried there will act up until they are acknowledged.

IN A RECENT CASE, A vacant property was left to a woman who had inherited it. Something would happen whenever she walked upon a certain section of it. She was left feeling ungrounded with deep sadness. When I checked into the property, it was not a burial site as I might have suspected, but it was a healing ground where injured natives were either healed or passed away of their injuries. These injuries were incurred when they fought to preserve their ancestral land. However, in most cases they were buried elsewhere. What was left behind was their sense of outrage, grief and sadness. In other words, there were soul fragments left there. I set about speaking with the fragments and discovered that the healing ground had hosted them between early 1754 and 1757. When I asked them which tribe they belonged to I heard a name that sounded similar to Oconee.

I knew it was unlikely they were Oconee but when I researched the area later it turns out the native tribe located there was Ocameechi, a name that was new to me. I then offered to move their fragmented selves either up to Great Spirit or to a place that was sacred to them, to which they readily agreed.

The client told me that the area now feels clear.

IN THE CASE OF SACRED burial sites, I manifest another plane of existence with my mind in which the burial site and sanctity are preserved in perpetuity. The land, in its present state can safely co-exist without interfering with the sacred site. I am unable to provide the reader with any rationale or methodology here, I simply 'knew' that this was possible.

Example

My temptation is to clear battle sites whenever I stumble across them, but I keep to Canadian sites unless I am asked to deal with sites outside my own country.

However, recently I assisted in clearing a site in Bull Run Ridge, Virginia. My assistance was requested by a man who lived there thus clearing my way to work on an American Civil War site.

There were two areas to clear. The first was a site where, again, natives who had been injured, subsequently died, and were laid to rest. It was not a sacred site as in a burial mound, but it was nonetheless sacred. They were placed in the shade under an older tree, most likely an oak, judging from the shape of it. When I lifted the site up to place it on another plane, I noticed that the long tap root of the tree was coming with it. When I looked further it was obvious that the tree was fully engaged in protecting the native spirits under it.

Given my work with the consciousness of trees, I shouldn't have been surprised. I was reminded to be more careful when dealing with the totality of nature at each site.

Now, I was free to clear the Civil War site there. I first saw the skirmishes, then noted a general for the Confederate side who presented himself. I asked him if he would marshal his remaining soldiers so that they could rejoin their families. He agreed. But when I approached the Union soldiers I had to guarantee their safety when they joined the Confederates. This was accomplished by explaining that the war had ended in their favour and that they were now in the wrong place. With the exception of a few men, they all agreed. The remaining resistant ones were held in place by the courage and commitments to their beliefs in the war. They had defined themselves by their beliefs and had to be cajoled to accept the reality of the outcome of the war.

It reminded me of the strength of belief and the lasting effect that has on soul fragmentation.

Eventually, they all left the battle site led by the Confederate general. This time, I thanked the plant life around the site for the protection.

What is most fascinating about this clearing event is that the person who requested my assistance felt an ancestral shift in his own body when the fragments were moved up. He felt physically lighter. I had accomplished the clearing remotely and told the client when I had worked on it. He felt it.

It is not often acknowledged that we all carry vestiges of the struggles our ancestors faced. It seems to be in our spiritual lineage.

Example

I was asked to check out a farmhouse that was experiencing trouble in the baby's room on the second floor. The baby often awoke very agitated at night and wouldn't settle down afterwards.

The owners had a sense that there was something else going on in the house. I was accompanied by a very gifted student of mine who was the initial contact with the owners. When I doused the main floor, it appeared to be clear. However, when I went up to the second floor it was a different story. In the front bedroom I 'saw' a tree growing in the centre of the room with a body hanging from a branch. I was confused until I asked about the history of the house.

Most early farmhouses in this area are either built at two separate times in a "T" shape or all at once. What was now the back part of the house, but appearing as an extension, had actually been built first. The front section was built later. There had been a tree where the front section was erected. Thus, my vision was correct. The suicide had happened before the front was added.

The man had felt overwhelmed by his life, never feeling quite good enough and a lack of success. There had been no resolution for him which is why he hung himself. Thus, his fretting soul fragment was stuck roaming through the house. After some conversation, I moved him up to Spirit or 'God' as was his belief. The house was now clear and the last I heard, the baby was sleeping well.

Example

I was asked to clear a house that a young family had just moved into. Their nanny had seen the apparition of a man walking around the second floor where the bedrooms were located. When I checked it out there were two spirits. One was a young man in a bright-coloured shirt who was indeed walking between one bedroom and another room that had been a large walk-in closet. The bedroom had been his and was heavy with sadness. The walk-in closet had been his Mother's and I felt a sense of longing there. The story that unfolded to me through him was that his parents were very busy socially and had ignored his emotional needs. He was going into the changing room as his parents were about to go out again for the evening. He was begging them not to leave him alone. He committed suicide I later found out, and there he was or rather his soul fragment was, still seeking his parents acknowledgment. I moved his soul up.

Then I found a second spirit sitting at the top of the servant's stairs. It was young girl about nine years old. She was dressed in a light blue party dress from the late 1940's or early fifties, with white socks and Mary-Janes on her feet. I sat down beside her and asked her why she was there. She told me that it was her favourite place to sit because she could hear the adults talking in the kitchen when her parents had a party. She was excited to tell me that children were moving into the house and she would have someone to play with. There was a large playroom on the third floor. I mentioned this to the new owner, and that her children would never feel alone in the house and would be happy there. To her credit, she told me that the spirit of the young girl could stay.

This is an example of a tortured soul fragment in the case of the young man, and a complete spirit in the case of the young girl. She was in her version of heaven and interestingly, she could see the future of children in the house.

Example

In the most astonishing case I have ever worked on, I had assistance. This was a magnificent, large historic house. The husband of the couple, who had recently purchased it, noticed odd sensations in the basement. He and his wife both felt a clearing was necessary. I toured around the house from the outside and took pictures. One window drew my attention. I then entered the house and did a preliminary scan. Then, with the owner's permission, I instructed a class I was about to teach, (coincidentally on clearing 'spirits'), to journey through the house remotely as part of the class using the pictures I had taken.

What the class found initially pushed the boundaries of my beliefs, but I have learned over the years to trust what comes.

This was a special class. Students and acquaintances of mine from more than twenty years ago were in it. People saw large society parties and gatherings on the main floor, with several hot spots I will refer to in a moment. The second floor had images of several children running about playing. In a bedroom was a man handcuffed to a bed and screaming in mental distress. Another student saw monkeys. Yes … monkeys.

In the basement they saw many spirits (soul fragments) of black people, and a tunnel that that ran out to the back of the property.

More than one student noted a connection to the Underground Railroad by which many black slaves had escaped to freedom in what was known as Upper Canada, now the province of Ontario. The escapees followed the railroads, paths and roads at night. There was, in fact, a railroad not far from the back of the property which was built in the latter years of the Underground Railroad.

The current owner confirmed that she had been told about a tunnel that had been closed up several years ago.

All of this information seemed too bizarre to be true. Three of the students were invited through the house with me a few days later. The woman who had seen the monkeys opened the door of a second floor bathroom to reveal new wallpaper had been installed … with monkeys on it! The door to that room had been closed when I first visited because a new floor was being installed.

I subsequently discovered that there was a history of mental illness (schizophrenia) in the original family. Thus, the image of the man handcuffed to the bed. I recall noticing my eyes fixing on the window of that room from the outside.

WHAT I FOUND IN MY own journey through the house prior to the students' exercise was that there had been sexual abuse of the service staff on the main floor by the original male owner. He had also committed sexual abuse of the black ex-slaves hiding in the basement. In all, I cleared twenty-six spirits from the basement of the house that day. It took me four days to recover.

After the three class members visited, I journeyed back a few days later to make sure we had cleared it completely. There were two further spirits in the basement now, which the class had seen, and one of a boy about six on the main floor. He was looking for his mother who had left by the front door. The boy was fathered by the original male owner of the house. His mother was a servant and had been banished when the wife of the household discovered the truth of the boy's paternity.

The two remaining soul fragments in the basement were originally outside workers on the estate. Why they were down there wasn't made known to me.

All three soul fragments were moved up and the young boy was finally reunited with his mother.

The house had been the location of many society parties both inside and outside on the grounds. Upstairs, children were watched over by a governess while the adults partied downstairs, thus the images that the class had noticed.

THE HOUSE WAS NOW COMPLETELY clear and the new family could make it theirs.

The class results were very impressive.

911

WHEN THE TRAGEDY OF 911 happened, I had just entered the lobby of the hotel in West Virginia where I stayed overnight. I noticed that everyone in the breakfast area was staring at the television. One of the twin towers had been struck and then I witnessed the second plane hitting the second tower. I immediately sensed that this was the work of Osama Bin Laden. I checked out, stopped at two ATM machines and took out the maximum I could. I was guessing that financial systems could be compromised and I wanted the insurance of cash in my pocket. I then headed to a Dairy Queen, picked up a large vanilla milkshake and continued onto the Blue Ridge Parkway. I figured that if the next thing I saw was a mushroom cloud, then I wanted a good view while sipping on a special treat from my childhood.

I was then on my way to Atlanta. As I drove, I wondered if I would be 'called upon' spiritually to assist those who were trapped and had died in the buildings. No call came. I continued driving.

In bed that night in Atlanta, a 'call' came. I journeyed to the site of the disaster and found a woman in her mid to late thirties who looked to be African American. She was wearing a jacket and blouse. She was completely covered in gray dust, alive but trapped by her legs and in total darkness. I could do nothing but hold her hand throughout the night to give her comfort.

In the morning, I shared with my hosts what I had been doing all night. Then, on the television came news that a survivor had been pulled out of the wreckage. It was that woman. She said that St. Peter had held her hand all night. I knew that most likely I wasn't the only one assisting and I was relieved to know she had been rescued.

But I was curious. Why hadn't I been called to help others? The answer came two weeks later when I returned home.

A healer had been staying in a hotel across from the twin towers for several days preceding 911. She noticed that whenever she looked across at the buildings, she saw spirits flying out of the windows and up into the sky. It made sense to me. Spirits leave and return to the bodies they inhabit for up to two weeks before death.

I can only assume that their spirits knew where they would be headed and therefore did not need a guide.

NEVER GIVE UP ON YOURSELF

WE ALL STRUGGLE WITH NEGATIVE influences and definitions of self from childhood into our early twenties. However, it is possible to change the resulting negativity as we choose to address the effect they have had upon our lives.

I considered suicide three times in my life, all within my first twenty-five years. Don't ever give up on yourself, especially if you feel weird, a mistake, depressed, a misfit and without hope. I am living testament to surviving those feelings and the erroneous perception of self they perpetuate. Self-love is one of the most difficult valuations to achieve yet, karma aside, it is our birthright.

No-one is without hope and possibility. Emotions hold the key to the transformation of that lack of esteem. Delve into them. Explore them. Get to know them. Pursue their character down to the belief of self that underlies them. Own them but don't let them own you. As with your brain messages, you aren't your emotions, you're the one who is reacting to them.

Never hesitate to see a mental health care professional.

It's invaluable assistance that can arm you with awareness and a whole lexicon of understanding that can inform the rest of your life.

A MORAL COMPASS

DO WE ASSIST PEOPLE TO live or to die? When we work with people who have a so-called terminal illness what is our role?

When you look at it in terms of its trajectory, life is a terminal condition. Yet, relatives, partners, siblings and children have a lot invested in keeping a loved one alive. When I am called in to work with someone whose vitality has been altered by disease or illness and the toxicity of some treatments, it creates a dilemma.

The pressure to participate in some form of miracle is palpable.

I might be the last hope, but the patient usually knows the truth. I try to get them alone so that I can ask them what they sense is really happening. More often my role entails bringing comfort, ease and honesty to a patient. The most difficult part is answering the questions of those around the patient without creating a sense of false hope.

It's a dance but the focus must be on the patient.

I sometimes make the distinction for them between healing and curing. Healing is assisting or promoting closure of a wound, either physical or emotional, that has characterized one's life.

And that healing can be fast, defying medical odds.

Example

In 1989, a friend of mine ran over his left foot with the rear tire of his bicycle when the front tire suddenly became wedged in a streetcar track in Toronto. This incident turned his foot back-to-front. The hospital said it was the worst compound spiral fracture they had ever seen. The x-rays showed that he had bone fragments located at the end of the bone near his ankle. That bone was now shorter than the one in his right leg. He phoned me and said: "*Get up here! We have two days to work on this.*"

I immediately headed over to the hospital and started working on his leg, stroking along the damaged bone to stretch it out.

Two days later he was wheeled into surgery and was wheeled out after only twenty minutes. A very frustrated surgeon walked briskly down the hall and into his room holding the X-ray.

"Look at this X-ray!" he said

"Clearly there are bone fragments present around the end of the bone. When I opened the leg up, the fragments were gone and the bone was perfect!" His legs were now the same length.

My friend didn't tell him why.

CURING ON THE OTHER HAND, is something that happens as the result of vaccination, for instance, or an intervention either surgically or medicinally so that the original issue can never return. For instance, we are often expected to "cure" cancer.

However, I will readily admit to having seen miracles occur, but it is a mistake to expect one.

People often assume that cancer is a foreign, invasive agent. In fact, our own cells have the propensity to convert to cancer. In terming cancer 'the enemy' we are then projecting hateful, aggressive messages upon ourselves. The mechanism of that conversion, at this point, is unknown to us but may have more to do with our own genes. Therefore, how we approach cancer is a delicate issue. In my experience, cancer often has an emotional relationship to unexpressed bitterness. If you cross-reference the concept of bitterness with the corresponding part of the body (*see* pages 14–16), a story may then emerge.

Incarnate life, that is your life in a body … is a one-way street.

Everyone gets to die but death need not be feared. We live as fully as we are capable of expressing at the time.

Then we leave our physical bodies behind.

However, our spiritual 'body' lives on.

Emotion that is not resolved in this life may be resolved in the afterlife but the focus I recommend is to resolve everything you can in this life because you may end up repeating those same issues in your next incarnation.

I have witnessed the spirits of people who have passed and are still tortured by what they did not accomplish or atone for in this life. Further, emotions that are suppressed in this life can often become the seeds of illness as the chart of my findings in England (*see* pages 1416) will attest. Nothing matters more in our lives than doing our own inner work.

If your outer life isn't working for you, chances are your inner life isn't working either. Get whatever assistance you need to manifest the highest, unencumbered version of yourself.

GRIEF

DO WE ASSIST PEOPLE TO grieve fully or to calm down and to move past their grief? It varies from person-to-person obviously, but of what is it an expression?

The overwhelming sense of loss and the accompanying emotion often obscure the presence and the belief in a spiritual life. If the person experiencing the loss is able to move back from the emotion momentarily, they will quite possibly notice that a familiar spirit is right with them. We define ourselves by the loss we find ourselves in, but that definition can limit our spiritual awareness.

Why can we not feel that presence as acutely as the physical? Did the spiritual life of a loved one perhaps also inhabit the body of those who are left behind? Is that the loss we feel?

Are they truly 'left behind' or are they just in the next 'room', metaphorically speaking? Can we then become more aware of them once we move beyond our own grief?

The more I have delved into spiritual existence, the less I am troubled by death. It may appear to be irreverent, but in my experience, 'passing over' is a true cause for celebration.

RESOLUTION

I AM IN MY TWILIGHT years. In truth, I welcome my exit from this plane of existence. I feel no urgency in hastening the termination, but I recognize that the signs and signals are now appearing. I live in an amazing town filled with fascinating people who have heart. These people will put themselves into community work out of a concern for their fellow beings. The measure of community service here is very high on a per capita basis.

I converse with complete strangers and discover that a story I share spontaneously has great import and fosters a profound connection between us. Yet, we were strangers a mere ten minutes earlier.

For the most part, I have kept my light hidden and do not share what I do unless I am specifically asked.

However, I now appear to be more visible to some strangers.

It feels akin to a farewell tour and is without any sense of remorse or regret but is instead full of gratitude, grace and ease.

I am surrounded by love and I feel blessed.

RESPONSIBILITY

THE RESPONSIBILITY I FEEL FOR this knowledge moves me to teach how to move this awareness across this planet. A planet that is our destiny to steward. What we do with this responsibility will affect generations of all manner of enspirited beings for millennia, but we must act quickly. As I write this, the world is again in danger of another war, one that we may not survive. However, I choose to remain hopeful.

> *"Never forget that you are one of a kind.*
> *Never forget that if there weren't any need for you in all*
> *your uniqueness to be on this earth, you wouldn't be*
> *here in the first place. And never forget, no matter how*
> *overwhelming life's challenges and problems seem to be,*
> *that one person can make a difference in the world.*
> *In fact, it is always because of one person that all the changes*
> *that matter in the world come about. So be that one person.* "
>
> — R. BUCKMINSTER FULLER

The future of this planet, the future of all beings, is up to us.

Which brings me to question whether my alien abduction experiences as a child and in my fifties were reminders that I have a specific responsibility. Does the fact that I can spontaneously catalyze healing in others mean that I have abilities and powers available to me that do not exist in all people? Have I made an error in assuming that my abilities are potentially universal in others?

My strongest mentor, the late Eleanor Moore, had a relationship to off-planet beings and 'created' spontaneous healing in others. Is it common in all people who have off-planet experience or do they have other responsibilities to the planet? I recently watched the documentary entitled "Witness Of Another World" which further piqued my fascination with the question of universality.

In meeting with the off-planet beings specific to my own experiences, I was told that "*I had agreed to this contract.*" Why was this contract in place? Am I an emissary or an agent of off-planet concerns for the planet? Am I just one of many?

My consciousness is awash in questions but not with many clear answers.

Obviously, my journey continues.

Bernard Morin

NOTES

I have resisted the writing about my work for years, primarily because of an old fear of humiliation or worse the expression of Ego it may foster. But it's also a resistance to creating a "How to" manual that may be held up as a rule or standard against which others are judged. Nonetheless, I have been urged forward in this endeavor by friends, students, clients and colleagues.

Reluctance, fear and suppression seem to be common themes in my life. As you will no doubt realize now that you have read the book, my reluctance was founded on an inner sense of unworthiness which connects all the stories.

The personal reason I commited to this reconstruction of my life is to give permission to those folks whose lives don't fit the 'norm', folks who feel isolated by their own experiences, fear and reluctance. The folks who feel 'weird' in their worlds.

ACKNOWLEDGEMENTS

There are innumerable people to thank for their support over the years. Not the least of whom are the late Eleanor Moore, Anita Levin, Rolf Erdmann, the late Sunny Cook, the late Mary Wachter and the late Henry Haasen. Without the experiences, the confidence and affirmation they fostered within me, this book would have no relevance. Also, my initial curiosity about our psychological states and the resulting physiological issues (subsequently termed psycho-neuro-immunology) was met and spurred on by the shared observations of a friend, Diana Chappell, in London, UK.

My students and clients over the years have provided me with the inspiration, experience, confirmation and curiosity that spills out here as knowledge. Cindy Fox, Paul Fox, Wayne Adam, Bob Strain, Francesca Warriner, Donna Harris, Sukoshi Rice, Mary Hamilton, Alice Teichert, Mike Katz, Hanna Lyons, Tamara Michael and Linda Ellis have supported me immeasurably over the years and are simply referenced as "friends" throughout this series of stories. They have been prodding me to do this project over many years, in particular Elizabeth Broomfield, who always seems to be able to see past my resistance. Also, my association with Dr. Paul Shenck over these many years has been invaluable.

Mark O'Connell, Katherine McHarg, Jeff Macklin, Jack Cain, Andrew Lawler, the late Chris Magee and Diane Dryden have all provided me with valuable editorial and graphic advice without which this book may not have seen the light of day. The very talented Greg Curtis assisted me in the creation of my logo and the graphic interpretations of the way I interpret the body. Finally and significantly, Tannice Goddard has been invaluable in breathing life into both the ebook and the print versions of the book. Her wisdom, overview, artfulness and expertise have been very timely gifts.

I am grateful to them all and feel humbled.

Manufactured by Amazon.ca
Bolton, ON